At Issue

Should Women Be Allowed to Serve in Combat in the U.S. Armed Forces?

Other Books in the At Issue Series:

At Issue

Should Women Be Allowed to Serve in Combat in the U.S. Armed Forces?

Diane Andrews Henningfeld, Book Editor

GREENHAVEN PRESS
An imprint of Thomson Gale, a part of The Thomson Corporation

THOMSON
™
GALE

Detroit • New York • San Francisco • New Haven, Conn. • Waterville, Maine • London

THOMSON
_____✳_____ ™
GALE

Christine Nasso, *Publisher*
Elizabeth Des Chenes, *Managing Editor*

© 2008 The Gale Group.

Star logo is a trademark and Gale and Greenhaven Press are registered trademarks used herein under license.

For more information, contact:
Greenhaven Press
27500 Drake Rd.
Farmington Hills, MI 48331-3535
Or you can visit our Internet site at http://www.gale.com

LIBRARY OF CONGRESS CATALOGING-IN-PUBLICATION DATA

Should women be allowed to serve in combat in the U.S. Armed Forces? /
Diane Andrews Henningfeld, book editor.
    p. cm. -- (At issue)
Includes bibliographical references and index.
ISBN-13: 978-0-7377-3938-1 (hardcover)
ISBN-13: 978-0-7377-3939-8 (pbk.)
1. 1. Women in combat--United States. I. I. Henningfeld,
Diane Andrews.
    UB418.W65W64 2007
    355.4082'0973--dc22

                                                    2007032721

ISBN-10: 0-7377-3938-X (hardcover)
ISBN-10: 0-7377-3939-8 (pbk.)

Printed in the United States of America
10 9 8 7 6 5 4 3 2 1

Contents

Introduction

On March 23, 2003, a U.S. Army support unit delivering supplies took a wrong turn in the town of Nasiriyah, near Basra, Iraq. The mistake proved costly. The unit was quickly surrounded and attacked. In all, eleven soldiers lost their lives in the ambush, nine were wounded, and seven captured.

News stories such as this one are not uncommon in any war zone. Certainly, soldiers who enlist in the Army and are sent into a war expect to be shot at, and even perhaps taken prisoner. The March 23, 2003, attack was different in one major respect: one of the soldiers captured was a woman, Quartermaster Corps Private First Class (PFC) Jessica Dawn Lynch.

News of Lynch's capture made the front pages of newspapers all over the United States, as did her rescue some nine days later, recorded on the Army's night vision cameras. Lynch became the focus of an intense media storm. As Lynch herself testified before Congress in April 2007, "My parent's home in Wirt County [West Virginia] was under the siege of the media all repeating the story of the little girl Rambo from the hills who went down fighting." Lynch's capture, rescue, and media response all serve to highlight some of the major issues facing a military that now has a significant number of women serving in nearly every role save one: Pentagon policy forbids the military to assign women infantry ground combat units.

The combat exclusion policy is the focus of intense debate among politicians, feminists, and the military. Several distinct issues drive the debate. The military has an urgent need to have more soldiers on the ground in Iraq in order to fulfill its objectives. As the number of men available for assignment shrinks, there is a growing need to place women in roles that they previously would not have held. Consequently, the Army has attempted to honor the ban on women in combat while still supporting combat troops by placing women in support units such as the one Lynch was in. Often the support units are connected, or "collocated," with ground combat troops.

This fact leads to the second important issue of debate concerning the role of women in combat. In wars such as the ones in Afghanistan and Iraq, it is increasingly difficult to determine where the front lines are. Lizette Alvarez, reporting for the *New York Times Upfront* in 2007, writes, "Pentagon policy officially forbids women, who make up 10 percent of American troops in Iraq and Afghanistan, from serving in combat roles. But the reality of the situation in both countries, where the front line can be anywhere, is making the rule hard to follow." Women serving in support units often find themselves being shot at and returning fire. As Spec. Xao Her told reporter Kevin Diaz in an article in the Minneapolis *Star Tribune* in May 2005, "When you're in Iraq, you're in a war zone. . . . We were under fire almost every week." Women have had ample opportunity to demonstrate valor under fire, according to General Frederick Kroesen. Writing about Sgt. Leigh Ann Hester, a Silver Star recipient, in an article in *Army*, he asserts, "Her performance earned a well-deserved recognition, but it also calls attention to the fact that other women are routinely earning Combat Action Badges for their solid professional performances under fire."

The third issue the Lynch case highlights is that of gender difference. Aside from the arguments concerning the physical capabilities of women, there is the question of whether the capture of a female soldier presents a greater opportunity for propaganda by the enemy. In March 2007, fifteen British sailors, including Leading Seaman Fay Turney were taken hostage in Iran. Major Judith Webb, writing in the English newspaper the *Daily Mail* argues, "The response of the public to the news that there was a mother of a three-year old child among the 15 hostages showed that however much we pretend otherwise, we are not capable of viewing a vulnerable female in the same way as her male counterparts." Likewise, Kathleen Parker, responding to Turney's plight, asserts in a much-quoted *Washington Post* editorial, "Positioning women to become pawns of propaganda . . . is called aiding and abetting the enemy." On the other hand, prisoners of war, regardless of gender, have historically been used for propaganda purposes. Senator John McCain was forced to sign a propaganda document while he was a prisoner of war during the Vietnam War, as were many other soldiers.

Lynch's 2007 testimony suggests one more troubling issue: to what end can women soldiers be used for propaganda within the United States? In the case of Lynch, her story was widely exaggerated and misreported, and even quickly turned into a made-for-television movie. Indeed, it was exposed as a media event, quite fictionalized. Lynch later denied most of what was reported about her heroics. She bluntly told Congress that she did not return fire and that the real heroes of the event were "people like [Pfc] Lori Piestewa and First Sergeant Robert Dowdy who picked up soldiers in harm's way. . . . The bottom line is the American people are capable of determining their own ideals for heroes and they don't need to be told elaborate tales."

The Lynch story connects with the way that the American public thinks about women and combat. As Sharon Cohen writes in the December 2, 2006, issue of *USA Today*, "The public, long accustomed to seeing disabled male veterans and grieving widows clutching folded U.S. flags, has adjusted to a new set of somber images: women soldiers coming home with life-changing injuries and tearful farewells to mothers, wives, and daughters." Nevertheless, while the public may be adjusting, the debate is not over. The viewpoints that follow answer, in very different ways, the question of whether women should be allowed to serve in combat roles in the U.S. Armed Services.

1

Women Should Be Allowed to Serve in Combat in the U.S. Armed Forces

J. Michael Brower

J. Michael Brower is an officer in the Oregon Air Guard. He has also served as an analyst in the office of the Secretary of the Army, located in the Pentagon, and as an immigration officer in the Department of Homeland Security.

A 1994 U.S. policy established that women cannot serve in ground combat units but that they can serve in support units placed ("collocated") with combat units. Women are serving on the front lines; therefore, they often find themselves in combat situations. Women have demonstrated competence in battle, and many have died. Consequently, women should be permitted in combat. They should also be given more combat training, credit for their contributions during combat, and equal opportunity for advancement in the military.

Women have been fighting shoulder-to-shoulder with men in the United States Army since the Republic's beginnings—undisputable historic fact. But many social conservatives are loudly complaining that clarifications, authored in 1994, concerning women in combat are being liberally interpreted thanks to operational necessity. They complain that American servicewomen are fighting openly alongside their brothers-in-arms in the global war on terrorism (GWOT).

J. Michael Brower, "Examining the Pros and Cons of Women in Combat," *The Officer*, vol. 81, no. 2, March 2005, pp. 38, 42–45. Copyright © 2005 Reserve Officers Association of the United States. Reproduced by permission.

Correct. Some of these armchair warriors claim that the Army wants to trash the current gender collocation policy [policy allowing women to serve in forward support positions, but not in combat positions] as part of an equalizing "social agenda." Incorrect.

Women are fighting and dying beside men—and will be— and there is nothing novel about it. Giving women credit where due, more training to defend themselves in firefights that find them, and making servicewomen equal partners in the armed forces—that would be new. As of mid-January 2005, 32 servicewomen have been killed in Iraq, five in Afghanistan, and more than 230 have earned Purple Hearts for combat wounds. . . .

Women's Roles Expand

The Army's internal discussions about collocation and mixed-sex Forward Support Companies (FSCs) are occurring *post festum* [after the event]. The Army has conceded in internal briefing papers reported by the *Washington Times* December 15, 2004, that "Army manpower cannot support elimination of female soldiers from all units designated to be units of action elements," and all-male FSCs are impossible because recruiting numbers are too small. A "scissors crisis" in recruitment—one blade expanding OPSTEMPO, [operations tempo] the other blade widening due to a diminishing human capital reserve for ground operations—has made women more indispensable to sustain PERSTEMPO [personnel tempo] levels. In his December 20, 2004, memo to the Army's chief of staff, chief of the Army Reserve LTG James R. Helmly has already warned that the Reserve "is rapidly degenerating into a 'broken' force." Helmly has requested more latitude in the area of personnel flexibility. With almost 1,500 troops killed in Iraq and more than 10,000 wounded, most since May 1, 2003 (when offensive operations officially ended), women have seen their roles expand in fact, but not in policy [statistics as of 2005].

With around 40 percent of warfighters in *Operation Iraqi Freedom* (OIF) and the Afghanistan campaign *Operation Enduring Freedom* (OEF) drawn from the Guard and Reserve forces, more focus has been placed on the rising sacrifices of the citizen-soldier. Use of the Guard and Reserve continues to grow in the face of the protracted insurgency in Iraq and continuing operations supporting OEF, which includes the hunt of 9/11 perpetrator Osama bin Laden. Hope remains that the recent elections in Iraq will decrease violence and restore security. In the meantime, who better than the National Guard's female leaders to assess the trajectory of servicewomen's participation in combat operations and the military generally?

[W]omen are indispensable in the search for suicide bombers.

Women Are Warriors

MG Jessica Wright, appointed to lead the Pennsylvania National Guard in early 2004, is the second woman in history to lead a state's National Guard. In a recent interview, she noted that women are serving all over the world, and are engaged in a "non-linear battlefield." Women are "operating in the same environment that our combat arms operate in. The important thing for our soldiers to remember is that whether you are mechanic or an infantryman, you are a warrior first," she emphasized.

Far from shying away from the opportunity that combat is offering, Wright says, "women serving in the military are warriors and I think that the current environment has provided them the opportunity to shine. Our 131st Transportation Company from Williamstown, Pa., was led by a female commander, CPT Laura McHugh, and a female first sergeant, Brenda Coston. That unit was very successful during combat," she noted.

Concerns over collocation rules and calls by conservative groups to keep women from the front lines are, in military terms, OBE [overtaken by events], though such calls have all but monopolized the mainstream media. The boom of operational necessity is a louder voice. Fall 2003's *Deployment Quarterly* features a female Marine on the cover, assault rifle at the ready, inspecting supply trucks in a combat zone near Al Faw, Iraq. This role is rule, not exception.

For instance, women are indispensable in the search for suicide bombers. "I also know that during many operations we need women to come along to search other females to preserve host nation sensitivities. So the role of women in warfare is expanding and I think it will mean greater opportunities for women in the future," General Wright observed.

Terrorist Killing Is Gender Neutral

Arguing the American culture does not accept women in combat and urging Americans to call for limiting women's ability to serve certainly has not had an effect on the terrorists—their killing remains gender neutral. "Some of our support units have attached personnel directly to combat arms battalions but this is only due to the non-linear battlefield that we are currently operating in. All units are operating out of forward operating bases and need support to be organic. Other than that, nothing has changed. The mission stays the same. However, as I said before, the role of women has expanded. For example, women have held the MOS [Military Occupational Specialty] of military police officer in the past, but our current mission has the combat arms branches performing a role closer to the mission of the MP," Wright explained.

CAPT Lory Manning, USN (Ret.), director of Women in the Military Project with Women's Research and Education Institute, agrees that women's roles are expanding, in spite of restrictive policies. Manning is the co-editor of the yearly report *Women in the Military: Where They Stand*. The GWOT has "helped military women 'win their spurs' so to speak. They have proven that they have the mental and physical endurance necessary, that they can handle themselves when under attack, and can live rough in the field," Manning says.

"What's going on in Iraq has certainly rendered moot the collocation policy the Army has used since 1994," Manning observed. "In 1994, the policy guidance to the services put out by the office of the secretary of defense stated the services could choose not to collocate women with units (below brigade-level) whose primary mission was direct ground combat," she asserted. The Army, then, has the option to collocate women with these units, and, strictly out of necessity, suffers the practice to continue, regardless of conservative kibitzing. Manning observed that "the Army is now choosing to collocate women with combat units at the battalion level as the 3rd Infantry Division redeploys to Iraq. So the situation in Iraq has certainly rendered the Army's 1994–2004 collocation policy obsolete." Instead of protecting women and training them for asymmetrical threats, some are more interested in ensuring that "traditional roles" for women are maintained despite operational needs. The phony *cause célèbre* [celebrated cause] over gender-based recruiting accounting for women's expanded roles discounts their bravery, patriotism and sacrifices.

Those who reject women's sacrifices in combat ignore the facts and prove that Churchill was right when he said, "Truth is the first casualty of war."

In the Real World, Women Are In Combat

MG Martha Rainville, America's first woman to command a state's National Guard, elected by Vermont's legislature for the first time in 1997, was also the youngest adjutant general in the country upon appointment. She agreed that although the "no women in combat" policy is being respected, it is impossible to practice in the real world. "Women are proving that they can and will perform their mission taskings as integrated members of their units. What has changed is the vulnerability of combat support and combat service support units, and the women assigned to them, to terrorist attack. Their response to attacks should reassure skeptics of women in the military."

Asked if the non-combat for women policy has withstood operational demands, or if a debate on the subject should he avoided, Rainville was adamant. "No, the debate is not moot. No, the policy has not withstood operational demands! We can assume that American forces will continue to deal with asymmetric warfare into the foreseeable future. It is time for our society to openly debate the role of the women and men serving in the military. Restrictions on one gender regardless of physical and mental requirements necessary for an assignment may no longer be desirable in today's society or even supportable in an all-volunteer force." Such a debate should be framed against the history of how women accord themselves in combat, assessed by the empirical facts, not the selected anecdotes.

Ignoring the Facts

Women are barred from 30 percent of active duty roles, including submarine, infantry, armor, artillery and Special Forces. Yet in the 1989 invasion of Panama, with more than 800 women participating, almost 20 percent came under fire—and returned fire. Nevertheless, quoted by the *Washington Times* in a page one story January 12, 2005, the president said, "There's no change of policy as far as I'm concerned. No women in combat. Having said that, let me explain, we've got to make sure we define combat properly: We've got women flying choppers and women flying fighters, which I'm perfectly content with." Bullets, RPGs, [Rocket Propelled Grenades] mortar rounds and IEDs [Improvised Explosive Device] will continue to decide when women are actually in combat, of course.

Those who reject women's sacrifices in combat ignore the facts and prove that Churchill was right when he said, "Truth is the first casualty of war." They refuse to mention the truth about Army Airborne CPT Kellie McCoy's Bronze Star earned in a firefight after she slew two of the enemy on September 18, 2003. Mockingly, McCoy dismissed the current policies on women in combat as *passé* [outdated]. "Our doctrine was suited for wars with front lines. In Iraq, the front line is everywhere," she told *The New York Daily News* December 14, 2004. America's Middle Eastern policy is best described as building a bicycle while riding it; similarly, our policy toward women in combat is to expand it in practice and cynically outlaw it on paper, primarily to keep top leadership roles male-only.

Guard members from Oregon, Vermont and Hawaii suffered more per-capita casualties in the GWOT than other states, sacrificing disproportionally due to their small populations. The Oregon Guard's highest-ranking woman and deputy chief of staff nevertheless agreed that the sacrifices have advanced female opportunities and accentuated their contributions. "I believe the GWOT has helped military women. They have deployed and served honorably," said COL Carol Brown, ARNG. "In a war like the one in Iraq, it doesn't matter if you are in a combat unit or a combat support unit, you may be subject to attack."

Brown concurred that operational reality is driving the exposure of women to combat. "Women are serving in combat service and combat service support units like transportation and logistic units. With the transformation of the Army, I believe the role or women in the military will expand and there will be greater opportunities for women." She added, "I believe women who are technically competent and physically capable can serve in any leadership role they want to."

Combat Experience Should Equal Advancement

When women do have combat experience, Rainville said opportunities for advancement in the military hierarchy should be equal. Asked what roles women who have combat experience should play in the military, she stated: "The same roles that are appropriate for men with combat experience: leader, trainer, mentor, diplomat, politician, citizen. We are already seeing women's roles expanded based on necessity. Our policies should reflect reality so that all involved know where they stand."

Women have acquitted themselves well in battle during the anti-terrorist campaigns of *Operation Enduring Freedom* and *Operation Iraqi Freedom*. Added General Wright, "More and more we see women appointed to a post that women have never held before. It's a growing trend and I believe that it will increase exponentially over time." As to expanding roles for women, Captain Manning agreed that "we certainly need to re-think the definition of ground combat with respect to insurgency. Too many people equate keeping women out of ground combat with keeping them out of danger—which has never been the intent." Intentionally restricting women from roles on paper that they can and do perform in fact, endangers them and their units, with the intent of cheapening their contributions and limiting their command potential. "The current operations in Iraq would not be possible without women," concluded Manning.

[C]ombat has found servicewomen in the global war on terrorism, and they have met the challenge with the requisite skill and fortitude.

Time to Recognize Reality

Lady "Liberty" leading the people with a bayoneted rifle and flag in Delacroix's famous 1830 French painting makes no impression on those arguing against women in combat. When anyone, not just women, get killed in war, we manifest a primal failing as a species. But as Rudyard Kipling observed, "The female of the species is more deadly than the male." That secret is out: We should urge our elected officials to recognize reality and women's abilities and contributions, and ignore the calls to ban women warriors from direct combat. Women need to be properly trained for an era that recognizes an end to traditional "front lines" and the ubiquity of asymmetrical threats. Technology has changed war in women's favor: cyberoffensives waged by *clickskrieg* [war waged by computer] often give women an edge on the digitized battlefield.

However, as Brig Gen Wilma Vaught, USAF (Ret.), Women in Military Service to America Foundation president, notes: "It's too late for this discussion. Women have been in combat and are in combat right now in Afghanistan and Iraq. They are in harm's way." When asked whether Americans' reluctance to send women into combat is a cultural bias against women being injured or killed in battle, General Vaught strongly disagrees. "Thirty women have been killed so far in action in Iraq. In some American cities, probably more women have been homicide victims during that same period." She believes women are safer in the military than in many places in the United States. This holds true especially in combat because they are part of a unit whose members always look out for one another.

Even the nominally conservative Martin Van Creveld commented in *The Transformation of War*: "The real reason why women are excluded [from combat] is not military but cultural and social." In brief, combat has found servicewomen in the global war on terrorism, and they have met the challenge with the requisite skill and fortitude. All that remains is to give them the credit for doing so.

2

Women Should Not Be Allowed to Serve in Combat in the U.S. Armed Forces

Phyllis Schlafly

Phyllis Schlafly is a lawyer and conservative political analyst who often writes on women's issues.

Placing women in units collocated with ground combat units is a violation of law. Women themselves do not want to be placed in combat units, and it is only ambitious feminists who want the law to be changed. Women are not physically capable of the demands of combat; thus, their presence on the battlefield endangers the troops and diminishes combat readiness. It is also likely that placing women in combat will make it more difficult to recruit male soldiers.

Why are our generals trying to push women into ground combat in Iraq despite Pentagon regulations and congressional law against it? What is it about civilian control of the military that the generals don't understand?

Current Department of Defense regulations exclude women from ground combat, as well as from assignment to forward support units that "collocate—i.e., are embedded side by side with units assigned a direct ground combat mission." Federal law requires that Congress be given 30 legislative days' advance notice of any change to this policy.

Army Secretary Francis Harvey has been skirting this policy by unilaterally rewording it to assign women to

Phyllis Schlafly, "Military Off Base in Sending Women into Combat," *Copley News Service*, May 26, 2005. Reproduced by permission.

forward-support units except when "*CONDUCTING* (emphasis added) an assigned direct ground combat mission." When a ground-combat unit actually engages the enemy, the women, who are slated to be roughly 10 percent of the forward-support companies, will have to be evacuated from the battlefield.

How many ground and air vehicles, and how many extra men, will this ridiculous plan require? Will the enemy hold fire until the evacuation is complete?

The Army's Devious Behavior

Frustrated by the Army's devious behavior, U.S. Reps. Duncan Hunter, R-Calif., and John McHugh, R-N.Y., had tried to add an amendment to the military appropriations bill to codify the current Defense Department regulations that the Army seems to have difficulty understanding. Feminists are lining up their media allies to demand that women be forced into land combat situations, while falsely asserting that Hunter-McHugh is "changing" the rule.

Much of the demand for women in combat comes from female officers who are eager to obtain medals and promotions. Enlisted women are acutely aware of the heavy lifting that must be done by combat infantry.

Denial of physical differences is an illusion that kills.

The Army's own opinion surveys prior to 2001 consistently reported that 85 percent to 90 percent of enlisted women oppose "being assigned to combat units on the same basis as men." Women enlistees have a right to expect the Army to obey current policy and law.

Advocates of women in combat say the front line is everywhere in Iraq. They continually try to fuzzy over the difference between being subject to risk, such as being ambushed by a car bomb, versus the task of aggressively seeking out and killing the enemy.

Army Chief of Staff Gen. Peter J. Schoomaker tried to laugh off the difference by saying that "maybe since we're killing 40,000 people a year on the highways, (women) shouldn't drive. That's very dangerous, too." Comparing the risk of highway driving with engaging the enemy in combat is insulting to our intelligence and common sense.

Women in Combat Will Lead to an Androgynous Society

Putting women in military combat is the cutting edge of the feminist goal to force us into an androgynous society. Feminists are determined to impose what Gloria Steinem called "liberation biology" that pretends all male-female differences are culturally imposed by a discriminatory patriarchy.

History offers no evidence for the proposition that the assignment of women to military combat jobs is the way to win wars, improve combat readiness, or promote national security.

No country in history has ever sent mothers of toddlers off to fight enemy soldiers until the United States did this in the Iraq war.

Women, on average, have only 60 percent of the physical strength of men, are about 6 inches shorter, and survive basic training only by the subterfuge of being graded on effort rather than on performance. These facts, self-evident to anyone who watches professional or Olympic sports competitions, are only some of the many sex differences confirmed by scholarly studies.

Denial of physical differences is an illusion that kills. That's the lesson of the March 11 courtroom massacre in Atlanta's Fulton County Courthouse. That's where authorities have returned a murder indictment against 6-foot, 210-pound Brian Nichols, a former college football player. Nichols is accused of overpowering a 5-foot-1, 51-year-old female sheriff's deputy, taking her gun and going on a crime spree that left four people dead, including the deputy, a judge, a courtroom reporter and a federal agent.

Every country that has experimented with women in actual combat has abandoned the idea, and the notion that Israel uses women in combat is a feminist myth. The armies and navies of every potential enemy are exclusively male; their combat readiness is not diminished by coed complications or social experimentation.

The 1992 Presidential Commission on the Assignment of Women in the Armed Forces voted to maintain the exemption of women from assignment to combat in ground troops, combat aviation, amphibious ships and submarines. But already 33 servicewomen, including mothers, have been killed and 270 wounded in the war in Iraq.

Women in Combat Hurts Recruiting

The Army is wondering why it can't meet its recruitment goals. It could be that the current 15 percent female quota is a turn-off to men who don't want to fight alongside of women who can't carry a man off the battlefield if he is wounded. Forcing women in or near land combat will hurt recruiting, not help.

No country in history ever sent mothers of toddlers off to fight enemy soldiers until the United States did this in the Iraq war. We hope this won't be the legacy of the Bush administration.

3

Women Already Serve in Combat in the U.S. Armed Forces Despite Ban

Ann Scott Tyson

Ann Scott Tyson is a Washington Post *staff writer.*

The official policy of the U.S. Armed Forces is that women may not serve in land combat roles, although women are serving in a growing number of important support positions in ground units attached to combat units. The women who serve in ground units are considered essential to the U.S. war effort. Because there are no front lines in this conflict and violence can erupt anywhere, these women often find themselves coming under fire, and often they return fire, in spite of the ban on women in combat roles. Women have demonstrated valor in combat and have been awarded medals for their bravery. Women are already serving with distinction in combat; therefore, many men and women believe that the official ban on women in combat is not realistic.

Jennifer Guay went to war to be a grunt. And the 170-pound former bartender from Leeds, Maine, with cropped red hair and a penchant for the bench press, has come pretty close.

It was mid-February and Guay, 26, an Army specialist who was the first woman to be assigned as an infantry combat medic, was spending 10 hours a day on missions with the 82nd Airborne Division, dodging rockets and grenades in the crowded streets of Mosul.

Ann Scott Tyson, "For Female GIs, Combat Is a Fact," *Washington Post*, May 13, 2005, p. A01. www.washingtonpost.com. Copyright © 2005, The Washington Post. Reprinted with permission.

"Break-break-break: U.S. soldier down!" a hard-edged voice came over the radio. A gun battle had just broken out.

In less than five minutes, Guay was at the scene. She dashed to Sgt. Christopher Pusateri, 21, who was lying on the ground, a bullet through his jaw. "I was in charge of this man's life," she recalled. Pusateri had "a massive trauma injury, and I had to get him off the middle of the street."

The Pentagon Policy Is Obsolete

Day after day, Guay has faced situations that would test the steel of any soldier. And female soldiers like her—as well as Army officers who support them—are seizing opportunities amid Iraq's indiscriminate violence to push back the barriers against women in combat. As American women in uniform patrol bomb-ridden highways, stand duty at checkpoints shouldering M-16s and raid houses in insurgent-contested towns, many have come to believe this 360-degree war has rendered obsolete a decade-old Pentagon policy barring them from serving with ground combat battalions.

"The Army has to understand the regulation that says women can't be placed in direct fire situations is archaic and not attainable," said Lt. Col. Cheri Provancha, commander of a Stryker Brigade support battalion in Mosul, who decided to bend Army rules and allow Guay to serve as a medic for an infantry company of the 82nd Airborne. Under a 1994 policy, women are excluded from units at the level of battalion and below that engage in direct ground combat.

"This war has proven that we need to revisit the policy, because they are out there doing it," Provancha, a 21-year Army veteran from San Diego, said from her base in what soldiers call Mosul's "mortar alley." "We are embedded with the enemy."

Dozens of soldiers interviewed across Iraq—male and female, from lower enlisted ranks to senior officers—voiced frustration over restrictions on women mandated in Washington that they say make no sense in the war they are fighting. All said the policy should be changed to allow, at a minimum, mixed-sex support units to be assigned to combat battalions. Many favored a far more radical step: letting qualified women join the infantry.

The Disconnect Between Washington and Iraq

But Congress is moving in the opposite direction. A House subcommittee, seeking to keep women out of combat, passed a measure this week [May 9, 2005] that would bar women from thousands of Army positions now open to them. In Iraq, female soldiers immediately denounced the vote.

"I refuse to have my right as a soldier taken from me because of my gender," Guay wrote in an e-mail. "It is my right to defend my country. . . . I am well aware of the danger. . . . Let me (us) do our job."

For many inside Army camps, the disconnect between Washington officialdom and the reality that female troops confront in Iraq was epitomized by President Bush's Jan. 11 [2005,] declaration of "No women in combat."

"That's an oxymoron!" said Sgt. Neva D. Trice, who leads a female Army search team that guards the gates of Baghdad's Green Zone, where many U.S. and Iraqi government facilities are located. "If he said no women in combat, then why are there women here in Iraq?"

"You can't tell me I'm not being shot at. You can't tell me I can't handle combat," said Provancha. . . .

Several male Army officers also dismissed Bush's statement as woefully uninformed. "The president got blindsided. The president didn't understand what the policy really was," said one officer, who requested anonymity because he was questioning the commander-in-chief. He and others urged Army leaders to push for new policies that reflect women's expanded role.

"I'm ashamed," he said, "that the Army has not taken this on."

Women Demonstrate Valor Under Fire

In sheer numbers, women are essential to the American military effort in Iraq—where tens of thousands have served—and are playing a bigger role than in any previous U.S. conflict. Historically, women's involvement in the military has surged in wartime. Today, that pattern is amplified by the all-volunteer U.S. military's growing share of women, which has steadily expanded in recent years to 15 percent of the active duty force.

Moreover, in contrast to their roles in past wars, women are serving in a widening variety of Army ground units—from logistics to military police, military intelligence and civil affairs—where they routinely face the same risks as soldiers in all-male combat units such as infantry and armor.

"We live and work with the infantry," said Maj. Mary Prophit, 42, who heads a four-person civil affairs team with a Stryker battalion in Mosul. An Army reservist and librarian from Glenoma, Wash., Prophit handles security duties from the hatch of a Stryker armored vehicle, watching houses during searches and returning fire when shot at. "Civil affairs teams have to be prepared to perform infantry functions, because at any time we could be diverted," she said.

In January [2005], Prophit was delivering kerosene heaters to a Mosul school when insurgents detonated a roadside bomb as her convoy passed, fatally wounding three Iraqi soldiers. Prophit moved to shield the medic treating the wounded, firing at insurgents who were shooting at them from a mosque across the street. "Women in combat is no longer an argument," she said matter-of-factly at her camp near the Mosul air field. "There is no rear area."

At least as often as insurgents attack all-male infantry forces, they strike targets such as military supply convoys, checkpoints and camps where U.S. servicewomen are often present. As a result, hostile fire in Iraq has taken a proportionally larger toll on servicewomen than in any prior U.S. conflict, killing 35 and wounding 279 [as of 2005].

"You can't tell me I'm not being shot at. You can't tell me I can't handle combat," said Provancha, who has nearly been hit by road bombs, rockets and the chow hall suicide bombing that killed 22 in December. "That was pretty frickin' direct fire if you ask me," she said, holding up a piece of shrapnel.

Many commanders in Iraq say they see a widening gap between war-zone realities and policies designed to limit women's exposure to combat.

Far from shrinking from the fight, women in Iraq are winning medals for valor under fire.

Spec. Shavodsha Hodges, 29, of San Antonio, says she joined the Army because her GI husband encouraged her to. She is a veteran of the 2003 Iraq invasion and well into her second year in a war zone. She and about 100 other women make up 20 percent of Provancha's logistics battalion in Mosul. They serve as truck and Stryker drivers, medics, mechanics and supply soldiers like Hodges who conduct between 50 and 70 convoy missions a month. Ferrying critical goods from Mosul to outlying bases on the precarious roads of northern Iraq, Hodges has developed keen instincts.

On Oct. 29 [2004], she was in a supply convoy heading out of the hostile town of Tall Afar, near the Syrian border. "We were told to watch out for an Iraqi national in black," she recalled. "Within seconds we were hit with an IED," or improvised explosive device, the military's term for a roadside bomb.

As her Humvee began to roll over, Hodges reached over and grabbed the legs of Pfc. Gregory Burchett, who was manning a .50-caliber machine gun. She pulled him down from the hatch and into the vehicle just before it flipped, saving him from being crushed.

Burchett was disoriented and moaning in pain. His face was bleeding from multiple shrapnel wounds and he couldn't move his arm. Hodges helped him out of the vehicle, but almost as soon they climbed out they came under small-arms fire from insurgents 200 yards away.

"Stay down!" Hodges yelled. Cradling Burchett's head in her lap, she lay forward over his upper body to shield him from the bullets. "Don't get up!" she said, twice sheltering the gunner from enemy rounds.

Meanwhile, the Humvee's commander, Staff Sgt. Armando Mejia, had his hand trapped under the vehicle. After the shooting stopped, Hodges and other soldiers pushed it up enough to free him. Only later did she realize that she, too, was injured.

For her quick thinking and bravery in the ambush, Hodges became the first woman in her brigade to be awarded the Army Commendation Medal with "V" device, for "valorous conduct" that "saved the lives of her fellow soldiers."

Between missions at her camp in Mosul, Hodges said she had no doubts about women's abilities in the war zone. "I think a woman is just as capable of dealing with this as a man," she said. "You think fast, and you react fast," she said, her tone confident but sober. "You have to be prepared at any moment, for anything."

War Zone Realities and Pentagon Policies

Many commanders in Iraq say they see a widening gap between war-zone realities and policies designed to limit women's exposure to combat.

Although the Army is barred from assigning women to ground combat battalions, in Iraq it skirts the ban with a twist in terminology. Instead of being "assigned," women are "attached in direct support of" the battalions, according to Army officers familiar with the policy. As a result, the Army avoids having to seek Pentagon and congressional approval to change the policy, officers said.

"What has changed? Nothing," said Lt. Col. Bob Roth of the 3rd Infantry Division. "You just want someone to feel better by saying we don't allow women in dangerous situations."

Male and female soldiers said many women in Iraq were performing well in risky jobs that require infantry skills.

A debate over the policy erupted in Washington last year [2004]. As the Army began reorganizing its combat brigades, the 3rd Infantry attempted to assign mixed-sex forward support companies to combat battalions. Capt. Christine Roney was on the verge of taking command of one of those companies when a soldier in her unit e-mailed Congress and opponents of women in combat. The Army reversed itself.

Eventually, the Army sidestepped the problem by making the forward support companies "attached" instead of "assigned," officers said. But Roney was nonetheless denied the job.

"A week before I was supposed to take command, they pulled me into the office and told me I couldn't be assigned," said Roney, of Loudonville, Ohio, now in Baghdad. "It was very disappointing." Instead, she was given a company in a noncombat battalion.

The Ban Should Be Lifed

Roney and other Army officers interviewed in Iraq agreed overwhelmingly that the Army's ban on locating female support soldiers with combat battalions was meaningless and should be lifted. The bigger question raised by the Iraq conflict, they said, is whether women should be allowed into combat units such as infantry and armor.

"I'm for it, because I think we can do it," said Pfc. Laura Springer, 20, of Odessa, Tex., one of only three women in her brigade licensed to drive the Army's Stryker vehicle. "At first all the infantry guys were staring at me. But I'm a good driver—I haven't hit anything—the same or even better."

Male and female soldiers said many women in Iraq were performing well in risky jobs that require infantry skills—from military police and civil affairs troops to female search teams that go on raids with Army and Marine infantry units. On raids, a woman is "as much infantry soldier on the ground doing the duties as anyone else," Roth said. "She may not have been the person who knocked the door in, but she's with the next stack getting ready to come in."

Most soldiers and officers interviewed also agreed that women need tougher physical fitness standards to perform well in infantry jobs, but that many could meet those standards. For some, the impact of pregnancy on readiness was a concern. Commanders of mixed-sex units in Iraq said that from 5 percent to 15 percent of their women became pregnant and did not deploy to Iraq, but one said health and family issues kept a similar percentage of men home.

Women Are Valuable in Combat Units

From Mosul to Ramadi to Baghdad, women such as Guay, who spent three months with the 82nd Airborne, have shown that they can be valuable players in combat units.

Guay was a student, engrossed by the moral dilemmas of war, when she decided to enlist in the Army in September 2002 to test her beliefs. "I called an Army recruiter. I wanted to be as grunt as possible," she said.

She lifted weights and studied combat medical skills. Once in Iraq, she actively sought missions "outside the wire" of the Mosul camp. When the 82nd Airborne arrived and needed a medic, Guay wanted to go. Provancha, whose team of medics is 40 percent female, assigned her.

"She wanted to be part of breaking the barrier down," Provancha said. Provancha took full responsibility for her decision, informing superiors rather than asking permission.

"Think of the fallout if she had gotten wounded or killed," Provancha said. "I probably would have been brought up on charges for defying Army policy." But that didn't happen. Instead, she said, Guay "did magnificently."

Initially, the 82nd questioned the move. At first, the grunts watched Guay. Then, in a casual sign of acceptance, they began calling her "Doc." A few firefights later, she became their "kick-ass medic." She was one of them.

"I was always working out and being strong and proficient," said Guay, proud of the fact that she could "out-bench some of the guys." She lived, ate and went on daily missions with the paratroops, bonding with the men whose lives could at any moment be placed in her hands.

When the soldiers fell, as Pusateri did in the firefight that gray day in February, Guay gave them her all, even when hope was slim. Recalling how she knelt at the mortally wounded sergeant's side, she said she would never forget being the last person with him, and the profound respect it engendered.

She quickly inserted an IV and ran a tube into his throat, pumping a bag every five seconds to put precious air into his lungs.

"Squeeze my hand," she told him. He did. She pumped the bag again. Pusateri was stable, but slowly losing consciousness. "You're so brave," she said, rubbing his head as everything around them faded into a blur. "You're amazing."

4

Women Demonstrate Competence in Combat Roles in the U.S. Armed Forces

Henry J. Cordes

Henry J. Cordes is a staff writer for the Omaha World-Herald.

The performance of women serving in the U.S. military in the wars in Afghanistan and Iraq demonstrate that they are capable of serving competently with men in combat conditions. Women are earning medals for valor at an increasing rate, including Combat Action Badges. Women also demonstrate in Iraq that they are steady under fire and capable of killing the enemy when they are attacked. The valor and gallantry shown by female soldiers under fire proves that the rules against women in combat will likely be changed.

When Army officials pinned a Bronze Star on Spc. Jenny Beck of Clarks, Neb., a week ago, they recounted her heroics during a harrowing convoy ambush in Iraq.

She showed exceptional valor and gallantry, the citation said, courageously dismounting from the safety of her vehicle to extract a fellow soldier trapped inside his, and then leading the convoy out of the kill zone.

In a broader view, that citation could also have mentioned what the Nebraskan and thousands of other U.S. service-women have accomplished in Iraq:

Writing a new chapter for women in the annals of U.S. military history.

Challenging long-held stereotypes of their mostly male counterparts.

Blurring distinctions the military has traditionally drawn between the sexes.

The Proving Grounds for Women Soldiers

The wars in Iraq and Afghanistan have served as major proving grounds for America's female soldiers, the first U.S. ground conflicts waged since a 1994 Pentagon edict opened most military jobs to women.

In the battle to secure Iraq, women such as Beck and fellow Nebraskans Jessica Hoelting Reed and Tricia Jameson have served side by side with men, often with distinction.

[R]oadside bombs know no gender.

"There's no doubt about it, unequivocally, they have proven they can do the job, be steady under fire and perform at an equal level to men," said Maj. Gen. Roger Lempke, commander of the Nebraska National Guard. "They have proven their mettle."

By rule, women in the U.S. military largely remain limited to "noncombat" support roles. They can't serve in infantry units or in support units based with such front-line fighters.

But in a war where the enemy is more likely to attack a support convoy than take on an infantry platoon, U.S. women in Iraq have fought, bled and died. While Washington policymakers continue to argue the intricacies of rules concerning women and combat, the reality in Iraq is overtaking that debate.

"Today's battlefield doesn't fit into nice little categories on paper," Nebraska Guard Capt. Craig Strong wrote in an e-mail interview from Iraq.

"We have combat units like the Marines a few kilometers from our 'noncombat' female medics, who are charged with going in to help them," he wrote.

And roadside bombs know no gender. The July death of Sgt. Jameson of Omaha, killed by an insurgent bomb as she went to the aid of wounded Marines, was a painful reminder of that.

More than 40 female soldiers—including two Nebraskans—have died in Iraq or Afghanistan, with nearly 300 wounded. [statistics as of 2005]

But perhaps more notable than the fact that U.S. women have been killed in Iraq is that they have killed.

When attacked, female soldiers have fought back and returned fire, believed to be a first in U.S. military history.

"No one knew how women would react when they have to shoot back. On the whole, they're doing very well," said Lory Manning, a former Navy officer now with the Washington-based Women's Research and Education Institute.

The situation in Iraq earlier this year prompted the chairman of the House Armed Services Committee to question whether the Pentagon was breaking its own rules and deploying female soldiers too close to front-line fighters.

Rep. Duncan Hunter, R-Calif., backed down after Defense Secretary Donald Rumsfeld argued that the changes Hunter sought would disrupt U.S. war efforts.

Elaine Donnelly, president of the Center for Military Readiness, a conservative group that wants women pulled out of harm's way, said the Pentagon has created unnecessary risk for women, including many who she said enlisted with no idea they'd be under fire.

"The cliche in Iraq is 'There is no front line,'" she said. "But there wasn't a front line in Vietnam, either, and we had nowhere near the number of women put at risk and dying like we have today. There was a reason for the rules, and there's still a reason for the rules."

Although women have served actively in the U.S. armed forces for more than a century, they mostly were limited to nursing and administrative roles intended to keep them far from the battlefield.

Today, women can fly any aircraft, including those that engage in direct combat. They generally can serve in any role on the ground other than those typically involved in a front-line offensive assault: infantry, armor, most artillery units and Special Forces.

Women have become an integral part of the all-volunteer U.S. armed forces, growing from 2 percent of overall strength in 1972 to 15 percent today.

They are playing a vital role in Iraq. Making up about 10 percent of the nearly 135,000 soldiers deployed, they drive trucks, repair vehicles and equipment, deliver emergency medical care and provide security.

[In 2005], Sgt. Leigh Ann Hester was awarded the nation's third-highest medal for valor, the Silver Star—becoming the first woman so honored for close combat.

Capt. Strong, the commander of Nebraska's 313th Medical Company, said that in his unit, a soldier is a soldier, regardless of gender.

Women make up almost half of his ground ambulance unit. One of those women—Sgt. Reed of Lawrence—recently was named Soldier of the Year by the *Army Times* newspaper.

Nearly every woman in Strong's unit is in line to receive the Army's Combat Action Badge—meaning they've been engaged by the enemy.

"I don't have the luxury to keep nearly half my medics inside the wire because they are female," Strong said. "Every one of them has performed their duty and did an outstanding job under extreme pressure."

Historically, the bar against women serving in combat had little to do with fear that they could be killed, said Manning, the former naval officer. She said it was because male soldiers didn't feel that they could rely on women, which could endanger their own lives.

But Manning said women have stood tall many times in Iraq, including during a massive March [2005] ambush of a Nebraska National Guard convoy.

Beck, the only woman on that convoy, was awarded the Bronze Star with Valor for her role in getting the stalled trucks moving again.

Two more women were among a force of 10 Kentucky National Guard Military Police who rushed to help, killing 27 insurgents. One of them, Sgt. Leigh Ann Hester, was awarded [in 2005] the nation's third-highest medal for valor, the Silver Star—becoming the first woman so honored for close combat.

The commander of the MPs told a reporter in Iraq the women "shouldn't be held up as showpieces for why there should be women in combat. They should be held up as examples of why it's irrelevant."

Women also appear to be standing up to the stress of Iraq's dangers.

A recent [as of 2005] Army study found that women serving as medics, drivers and mechanics in Iraq showed no more incidence of post-traumatic stress or depression than male counterparts.

Many now believe that the showing of women in Iraq will force the Pentagon to again examine the role of female soldiers, although no one seems to suggest that infantry units will be opened to women anytime soon. It's a fact women aren't as physically strong, said the Nebraska Guard's Lempke, and there are times in combat where strength matters.

Manning, of the Women's Research and Education institute, said restrictions on the basing of female support soldiers directly with front-line infantry likely will fall. She also thinks the public supports a wider role for women.

"I hear from a lot of veterans who are very admiring of their gallantry. They're saying, 'You go, girl.'"

5

Physical Differences
Make Women Incompetent
in Combat Roles

Mackubin Thomas Owens

Mackubin Thomas Owens is an associate dean of academics and a professor of national-security affairs at the Naval War College in Newport, RI.

Women should not be placed in ground combat roles nor should they be placed in forward support companies (FSCs). The rationale for this is that women are not physically large enough or strong enough to handle the necessary equipment. In addition, double standards result from the physical differences between men and women, as well as sexual competition, male protectiveness, and favoritism. Although women serve bravely in support roles, their physical limitations render them unfit for combat.

Last year [2004], the U.S. Army redesigned its combat brigades into "units of action": task-organized, self-contained organizations that include support troops—or forward support companies (FSCs)—embedded within them. The change was designed to make our troops more rapidly deployable. Unfortunately, it has been adulterated by a bow to political correctness that threatens to attenuate the military's effectiveness.

Current regulations prohibit women from ground combat—a prohibition that also applies to women in FSCs. Never-

Mackubin Thomas Owens, "GI Jane, Again: The Army Tries to Sneak Women into Combat, and Some Congressmen Try to Stop It." *National Review*, June 6, 2005. Copyright © 2005 by National Review, Inc., 215 Lexington Avenue, New York, NY 10016. Reproduced by permission.

theless, the Army, claiming that there are not enough men to fill positions in the FSCs, has begun to assign women to them. Army leaders claim that this change is consistent with current regulations, and that Defense Department rules bar women from FSCs only during moments in which those units are "conducting" combat. The implication is that women would be withdrawn from them before the onset of hostilities.

House Armed Services Committee chairman Duncan Hunter (R., Calif.) is not amused by this novel interpretation. Accordingly, he asked Rep. John McHugh (R., N.Y.) to introduce an amendment to the defense-authorization bill that bars women from serving in FSCs. This legislative effort is well founded. There are good reasons for women not to be involved in ground-combat support.

To understand these reasons, one must understand that the fundamental nature of war, so well described by Carl von Clausewitz 170 years ago, has not been significantly altered by technological advances. It is still, as Clausewitz wrote, a complex phenomenon, highly influenced by chance and uncertainty.

The female soldier is, on average, about five inches shorter than the male soldier. She has half the upper-body strength, lower aerobic capacity, and 37 percent less muscle mass.

An important element of war is "friction," which Clausewitz described as "the only concept that more or less corresponds to the factors that distinguish real war from war on paper." Clausewitz used the term "friction" to describe the cumulative effect of the small, often unnoticeable events that are amplified in war, producing unanticipated macro-effects:

Countless minor incidents—the kind you can never really foresee—combine to lower the general level of performance, so that one always falls far short of the intended goal. . . . The military machine—the army and everything related to it—is basically very simple and therefore seems easy to manage. But we should keep in mind that none of its components is of one piece: each part is composed of individuals . . . the least important of whom may chance to delay things or somehow make them go wrong. . . . This tremendous friction, which cannot, as in mechanics, be reduced to a few points, is everywhere in contact with chance, and brings about effects that cannot be measured, just because they are largely due to chance.

The military tries to reduce the natural friction of combat through training, discipline, regulations, orders, and what Clausewitz calls "the iron will of the commander." One particularly important way of countering friction is to promote unit cohesion. Unit cohesion in combat is far more than just "teamwork." Cohesion arises from the bond among disparate individuals who face death and misery together. This bond is akin to what the Greeks called philia—friendship, comradeship, or brotherly love.

Every service has lower physical standards for women than for men.

There is substantial evidence to suggest that the presence of women in combat would undermine unit cohesion and thereby increase friction. Indeed, friction resulting from the presence of women in the military has already manifested itself in three ways: problems arising from physical differences between men and women; the emergence of double standards that result from these physical differences, undermining fairness and trust; and the replacement of philia by eros. All of these factors undermine morale and may lead to failure on a future battlefield.

As I wrote in these pages in December, a major source of increased friction is traceable to innate differences between the bodies of men and women. A partial catalogue of these differences would include the following facts: The female solider is, on average, about five inches shorter than the male soldier. She has half the upper-body strength, lower aerobic capacity, and 37 percent less muscle mass. She also has a lighter skeleton, which leads to a higher incidence of structural injuries than among men. These differences have had an adverse effect on the U.S. military's effectiveness. They are also excellent reasons to keep women out of FSCs. Women may be able to drive five-ton trucks, but need a man's help if they must change the tires. Women can be assigned to a field-artillery unit, but often can't handle the ammunition. These are exactly the sorts of physically demanding jobs a mechanic in an FSC would be expected to perform.

Second, the physical differences between men and women have generated a series of undeniable double standards in the military. In practice, the desire for equal opportunity usually becomes a demand for equal results, and brings about a watering down of standards in order to accommodate women's generally lower physical capabilities. No one can deny that "gender norming" is widespread in the military. In fact, every service has lower physical standards for women than for men.

Unfortunately, this practice undermines morale by attacking the crux of the military ethos: fairness. Such double standards cause resentment in many military men, a resentment that leads to cynicism about military women in general—even those who have not benefited from a double standard and are performing their duties with distinction.

Finally, one consequence of having men and women live in close proximity under battlefield conditions is to unleash eros on an institution that depends for success on philia. Unlike philia, eros is individual and exclusive. Eros manifests itself as sexual competition, male protectiveness, and favoritism. As former secretary of the Navy James Webb has observed, "[T]here is no greater or more natural bias than that of an individual toward a beloved. And few emotions are more powerful, or more distracting, than those surrounding the pursuit of, competition for, or the breaking off of amorous relationships."

Only a feminist ideologue (or a P.C. military officer) would deny the destructive impact of such relationships on unit cohesion. Does a superior order his or her beloved into harm's way? What happens to morale and unit cohesion when the superior demonstrates favoritism toward the beloved? What about when jealousy rears its head? And what about the possibility that favoritism will be perceived, even when it does not exist?

Social engineering cannot change the fact that men treat women differently than they treat other men. Research shows that romantic relationships among co-workers do not enhance efficiency, and in many cases adversely affect morale and teamwork. But while lives are not at stake in the civilian workplace, they are at stake in military combat.

Of course, there have been incidents in Iraq in which women have performed well in a combat emergency. The mainstream media have tended to fixate on these incidents. *ABC News* aired a story in March [2005] about a woman in a National Guard military-police unit, and the *Washington Post* had a similar piece after a House subcommittee voted to bar women from FSCs. But such isolated cases don't refute the general argument that widespread assignment of women to combat units would be dangerous because of its impact on unit cohesion and morale.

Apart from questions of the military's effectiveness, there's one last issue to consider: By and large, most women in the Army and the other services don't want to be assigned to combat units or the support units embedded with them. If the Army is worried about not being able to recruit enough women, then putting women on the slippery slope to combat assignments surely isn't the best way to solve the problem.

As Elaine Donnelly of the Center for Military Readiness has remarked, the question of women in combat is not a "women's issue"; it is a national-security issue. That's something we should all be concerned about—and Congress is right to get involved.

6

The Combat Exclusion Law Is Unconstitutional and Should Be Struck Down

Valorie K. Vojdik

Valorie K. Vojdik is a law professor at West Virginia University College of Law.

The U.S. Supreme Court must be persuaded that the exclusion of women from combat is part of a larger system of gender subordination, rather than a simple stereotyping of women. The military emphasizes the difference between men and women in order to maintain the superiority of men. The military perpetuated a similar system of subordination when they maintained a policy of racial segregation. When viewed in this light, the ban on women in combat is a means to maintain the inequality of women. The law denies women equal citizenship status with men; therefore, it is unconstitutional and should be changed.

Rather than focus solely on the military's stereotypical judgments of women's abilities, a more persuasive approach would seek to persuade the courts that the combat exclusion is part and parcel of an institutional system of gender subordination. Through a range of institutional practices, the military as an institution constructs men and women as fundamentally different, rationalizing the exclusion of women even when their courage under fire continues to be demonstrated. The refusal of military leaders to open their ranks to

Valorie K. Vojdik, "Beyond Stereotyping in Equal Protection Doctrine: Reframing the Exclusion of Women from Combat," *Alabama Law Review*, vol. 57, no. 2, Winter 2005. Copyright © 2005 by Alabama Law Review. Reproduced by permission of the author.

qualified women does not rest on mistaken judgments about their capabilities, but upon a deep-seated hostility toward females that is institutionalized through a range of social practices that privilege masculinity and demean femininity.

As [legal scholar Kenneth] Karst has argued, the combat exclusion operates the same as the historical exclusion of blacks from all-white units, which reinforced the racial subordination of blacks, and the exclusion of gays from military service. Like the military's now-discredited policy of racial segregation and its current ban on homosexuals, the categorical exclusion of women from direct ground combat rests upon invidious social distinctions between the privileged male warriors and the outsiders. Such distinctions create a caste system underlying a social belief that the outside group is inherently different from, and inferior to, the men who are warriors.

Kenneth Karst has argued eloquently that the exclusion of women from combat preserves the ideology of masculinity or "manhood," rationalizing male access to power. Karst argues that the combat exclusion "symbolizes and reinforcees a traditional view of femininity that subordinates women." The exclusion of women is essential to enforce the bounds of gender that maintain separate spheres within the military—males as warriors, females as support personnel.

The Warrior as Masculine

Masculinity is not merely an ideology or belief, however, but a social practice within the military that constructs warriors as male and masculine. As [French sociologist Pierre] Bourdieu argues, masculinity as a social practice rationalizes the inequality and subordination of women within the military and society. Warriors are gendered male and masculine. The military traditionally has considered basic training a "proving ground" for masculinity. Recruiting slogans for the military have featured slogans such as "The Marine Corps Builds Men" and "Join the Army and Feel Like a Man." Recruiting advertisements historically have focused on challenging boys to become men. For example, an advertisement for the Army National Guard in the late 1980s was captioned "kiss your momma goodbye" and featured a photograph of a group of men wading through deep water. As recently as 2004, the Air Force Academy boasted a large sign that read, "Bring Me Men."

As [writer Joshua] Goldstein argues in *War and Gender*, the relationship between gender and war is reciprocal: Warriors are constructed as masculine, and masculinity is constructed through war. According to David Marlowe, the chief of Military Psychiatry at the Walter Reed Army Institute of Research, "the soldier's world is characterized by a stereotypical masculinity. His language is profane, his professed sexuality crude and direct; his maleness is his armor, the measure of his competence, capability, and confidence in himself." . . .

By highlighting the gender of female cadets, the military enforced gender distinction within the military.

The integration of women into the highly masculinized military culture fundamentally challenges the constructed identity of the warrior as male and the military as masculine. As retired Navy admiral James Webb explains, the military historically provided a "ritualistic rite of passage into manhood." According to Webb, the integration of women into the military makes male troops "feel stripped, symbolically and actually." Webb argued that the inclusion of women will disrupt the link between warfare and masculinity and reduce men's motivation for combat. He stated, "The real question is this: Where in the country can someone go to find out if he is a man? And where can someone who knows he is a man go to celebrate his masculinity?" As [law professor] Kingley R. Browne explains, "If combat is no longer a 'manly' pursuit, then failure at it is no longer a failure of manhood."

The opposition of those male officers and members of the Joint Chiefs of Staff who testified against women in combat in congressional hearings, illustrates this attitude. Though couched in terms of unit cohesion and effectiveness, their testimony reflects the underlying belief that a warrior is valuable precisely because women cannot do it. As a first sergeant in Special Operations testified, "The warrior mentality will crumble if women are placed in combat positions. . . . There needs to be that belief that 'I can do this because nobody else can.'" A female Air Force pilot testified before the commission that a male in test pilot school told her, "'Look, I can handle anything, but I can't handle being worse than you.'" Marine colonel Ron Ray testified, "Why do these women want to trade the best of what it means to be a woman, for the worst of what it means to be a man?" Even more bluntly, General [William] Westmoreland testified against the repeal of the combat exclusion laws in 1979, stating, "no man with gumption wants a woman to fight his nation's battles."

Highlighting Femininity

Because of the fundamental challenge that women pose to the identity of the warrior as male and masculine, the military has responded to the integration of women through a range of practices that highlight the femininity of female troops and thereby preserve the boundaries of gender within the military as an institution. One fascinating example is the military's adoption of numerous dress and grooming codes that compelled female cadets and service members to appear socially feminine.

The Marine Corps responded to the integration of females by preserving visible distinctions between male and female Marines. The Marine Corps insisted on calling its females "Women Marines," or "WMs." Other terms for females used in the Corps were more derogatory, such as "BAMs or Bammies (an acronym for 'Broad-Assed Marines') and Marionettes."

These terms distinguish females as different from, and inferior to, "real" Marines, who are male. To further enforce the gender distinction, the Marine Corps required female recruits to wear makeup—at a minimum, lipstick and eye shadow. Female recruits were also required to attend classes on makeup, hair care, poise, and etiquette. The Air Force Academy required that women's uniforms make apparent the gender distinction between male and female cadets; female cadets were required to look "feminine." At West Point, the academy initially banned female cadets from wearing skirts to a school dance, only to reverse itself after observing "'mirror-image couples dancing in short hair and dress gray trousers.'" West Point also required the first class of female cadets to attend a lecture on make-up application sponsored by Revlon, the cosmetics manufacturer.

The sexual harassment and assault of military women sends the message that female troops are sexual objects, not warriors.

By highlighting the gender of female cadets, the military enforced gender distinction within the military. Rather than include women as warriors, the military symbolically separated females from the "real" male warriors, preserving the masculinity of warriors and the hierarchy of gender within the institution.

Pervasive Sexual Harassment

The integration of women into the military's hyper-masculine culture has also resulted in widespread hostility and harassment of those women who transgress the boundaries of gender. Sexual harassment of military women is pervasive. According to a 1995 Department of Defense study, nearly 70% of military women have experienced sexual harassment in their workplace. An Army senior review panel similarly reported in 1997 that 80% of men and 84% of women in the Army reported experiencing inappropriate harassment such as "crude or offensive actions, sexism, unwanted sexual attention or more serious problems like assault." The sexual harassment and assault of military women sends the message that female troops are sexual objects, not warriors; harassment thereby polices the boundaries of gender within the military.

The admission of women into the federal service academies in the 1970s has been met with similar hostility and harassment. The last all-male class at West Point declared themselves the "Last Class with Balls" and posed for a yearbook photograph holding all sorts of balls, including footballs, basketballs, and baseballs. . . .

More than twenty years after the admission of women, sexual abuse and harassment of females at the federal service academies continues to be substantial. Following the well-publicized reports in 2003 of the raping of Air Force female cadets, a survey by the Defense Department inspector general found that 19% of female cadets at the Air Force Academy said they had been assaulted while at the academy. Half of the women attending the Navy, Air Force, and Army service academies reported being sexually harassed on campus. In March 2005, the Department of Defense released a report documenting that one out of seven women in the federal service academies surveyed reported that they had been sexually assaulted by their male peers.

In July 2005, the Department of Defense Task Force on Sexual Harassment and Violence in Military Service Academies concluded that the harassment and violence were partially rooted in the devaluation of women in the military. Despite the fact that women have been at the academy for over twenty years, DOD reported that one out of four male cadets surveyed reported that women do not belong at the Air Force Academy. The report cited the persistence of "hostile attitudes and inappropriate actions toward women, and the toleration of these by some cadets and midshipmen," as interfering with a safe environment to create new military leaders. The Task Force specifically recognized that the continued exclusion of women from "highly regarded combat specialties" fosters an environment of hostility and harassment. The sexual harassment and assault of military women sends the message that female troops are sexual objects, not warriors.

The combat exclusion constructs and preserves a gendered system of labor that reflects and perpetuates male supremacy and female subordination.

Violence toward female troops by their male officers and peers is similarly widespread. In a 2003 report by the Iowa City Veterans Affairs Medical Center, one-third of former military women treated by Veterans Affairs medical centers reported suffering rape or attempted rape during their military careers. Fourteen percent said they were gang-raped by co-workers. One in five women who reported being raped said they believed "rape was to be expected in the military." ...

Most recently, U.S. female troops in the U.S. Central Command's theater of operation in the Middle East, including Iraq and Afghanistan, have reported 112 incidents of rape, assault, and other forms of sexual misconduct during an eighteen-month period from August 2002 through February 2004. The official number of reports likely understates the actual number of assaults because many women are reluctant to report such incidents, fearing reprisal. The Miles Foundation, a nonprofit group that assists soldiers who have been sexually assaulted, has received 307 reports of sexual assault from soldiers serving in Iraq, Afghanistan, Kuwait, and Bahrain—most of whom were female.

Beyond Stereotyping

By moving beyond stereotyping, the argument against judicial deference to the military's discriminatory policy becomes substantially stronger. As Judge Fletcher observed in *Philips v. Perry*, judicial deference to a military policy that is based upon hatred of, and prejudice toward, an excluded class of people is unjustified. As Kenneth Karst has argued, the institutional opposition to women in direct ground combat is no different than the military's former policy of excluding African-Americans or homosexuals. While each involves a classificatory scheme, each enforces a status hierarchy that preserves the military for white, heterosexual males.

[O]pening the doors to women in combat fundamentally challenges the myth of masculinity.

The harassment and violence toward military women illustrates the persistent hostility and denigration of female troops. By shifting the focus from gender stereotyping to the institutional practices within the military that construct warriors as male and masculine, the direct ground combat exclusion appears less like a mistake in classification and more like a fundamental means of enforcing the status of military women as second-class citizens. The military's discriminatory policy, like the use of gender-based peremptory challenges in *J.E.B. v. Alabama* perpetuates the historical exclusion of women from the military and stigmatizes women as different and inferior, unworthy of the role of warrior.

The combat exclusion constructs and preserves a gendered system of labor that reflects and perpetuates male supremacy and female subordination. In this sense, the combat exclusion functions in the same way as the anti-miscegenation laws [laws against interracial marriage] struck down by the Supreme Court in *Loving v. Virginia*. In *Loving*, the Supreme Court relied on its anti-subordination doctrine to strike down Virginia's anti-miscegenation law as violating the right to equal protection. The Court rejected the notion of formal equality advanced by the state defendant that the law prohibited interracial marriages by both blacks and whites and therefore was racially neutral because it treated all persons equally without regard to their race. Prohibitions against interracial marriage, the Court held, were part and parcel of maintaining a system of racial distinction that perpetuated the subordination of blacks under the law. Like the anti-miscegenation statute in *Loving*, the categorical exclusion of women from direct ground combat demeans and stigmatizes women as different and inferior.

A legal challenge to the combat exclusion, as illustrated above, does not merely vindicate the goals of formal equality. The constitutional wrong is not simply that the military has mistakenly concluded that no woman is capable of engaging in combat (although the exclusion clearly reflects overly broad gender stereotypes), but that the military, through a range of institutional practices, constructs and preserves a gendered caste system. By making the military as an institution visible, the hostility toward women as a group becomes plain to see. Rather than accept the military's gender norms, opening the doors to women in combat fundamentally challenges the myth of masculinity inside one of the most powerful institutions that continue to deny women equal citizenship status.

The Combat Exclusion Law for Women Must Be Enforced

Elaine Donnelly

Elaine Donnelly is a former member of the 1992 Presidential Commission on the Assignment of Women in the Armed Forces and President of the Center for Military Readiness.

U.S. Department of Defense regulations require that all fighting battalions and their support units should be comprised entirely of men; however, Secretary of Defense Donald Rumsfeld is not adequately ensuring that the regulation is fully enforced. As a result, women are serving in units collocated with combat units and are coming under fire, to the detriment of themselves and the men who serve with them. Rumsfeld and President George W. Bush must support the troops by insisting that military leaders follow the law.

Retired generals have fired volleys at Donald Rumsfeld, but he will stay as Secretary of Defense [Rumsfeld resigned November 6, 2006). This is only fair, since Rumsfeld should have to deal with the consequences of problematic personnel policies that were set in motion on his watch.

Under Rumsfeld, social engineers have accelerated their agenda. Rumsfeld is known for abrading subordinates, but not Army officials who continue to violate policy and law on the issue of women in land combat.

All deployed soldiers, men and women, are serving "in harm's way." But even without a "front line," the missions of

Elaine Donnelly, "Rumsfeld Dithers on Women," *Human Events (www.human events.com)*, April 27, 2006. Reproduced by permission.

direct ground combat units have not changed. Infantry, armor, and Special Operations Forces attack the enemy with deliberate offensive action under fire. These fighting battalions, and support units that "collocate" with them 100% of the time, are required by Defense Department regulations to be all male.

If the Army wants to change the "collocation rule," the secretary of defense must approve and formally report the change to Congress approximately three months (30 legislative days) in advance. The law also requires an analysis of proposed changes on young women's exemption from Selective Service obligations.

These requirements have not been met, even though the Army has placed female soldiers in formerly all-male support units that collocate with infantry/armor battalions in the Third and Fourth Infantry, 101st Airborne, and First Cavalry divisions.

Even if the Army had sufficient resources to evacuate women on the eve of battle, the disruption could cause missions to fail and lives to be lost.

Women Are in Units that Should Be All Male

Army Secretary Francis Harvey denies a need to inform Congress of such assignments—but there is a "catch." Female soldiers are administratively "assigned," on paper only, to legally open (brigade level) units. In reality they are placed in "attached" forward support companies that collocate with land combat battalions, and are required to be all male.

Secretary Harvey has claimed that female soldiers will be removed (somehow) when battalions begin "conducting" or "performing" direct ground combat. Even if the Army had sufficient resources to evacuate women on the eve of battle, the disruption could cause missions to fail and lives to be lost.

Where is Congress on this? In 2005 House Armed Services chairman Duncan Hunter (R.-Calif.) conducted an investigation, and led the first major debate on women in combat in 15 years. Army officials initially denied illicit assignments, but later used semantics and sophistry to justify them. Dissatisfied members of Hunter's committee passed legislation to codify current Defense Department regulations.

Substituting women for men in combat-collocated support units increases danger for everyone.

Instead of issuing a swift order to bring the Army back into line, Rumsfeld persuaded Hunter to withdraw his legislation. A substitute amendment in the 2006 Defense Authorization Act mandated a detailed report on women in land combat, due on March 31, 2006. Rumsfeld's office ignored the deadline and diverted the task to RAND Corporation [a nonprofit research institution] which will not produce a report until December 31 [2006]. If a Democratic administration displayed such contemptuousness, Republicans would be up in arms.

But congressional oversight on matters affecting women in the military should not be a partisan matter. Some legislators on both sides of the aisle are taking this issue seriously, but most seem unconcerned about the consequences of decisions being made by default.

The Ban on Women in Combat Must Be Upheld

The cost of doing nothing starts with confusion among soldiers who are beginning to doubt the judgment of their leaders. No one has provided data proving shortages of men for the combat arms, but deficiencies could occur if the institu tional Army continues to supply CENTCOM [Central Command] with an unsuitable "inventory" of soldiers who are not eligible for the infantry.

Substituting women for men in combat-collocated support units increases danger for everyone. Female soldiers are brave, but proximity matters. In combat collocated units soldiers need to be strong enough to individually lift and evacuate a wounded infantryman under fire.

When feminists demand "career opportunities" in infantry battalions, how will Rumsfeld respond? The devil is not in the details, but in the priorities used to determine policy. If career considerations are paramount, incremental changes will increase demands for "consistency" in Army and Marine infantry, armor, and Special Operations Forces. And if the land combat notification law is not enforced, a similar one regarding female sailors on submarines has no meaning either.

Enter the ACLU [American Civil Liberties Union], which will file another lawsuit challenging male-only Selective Service registration. The Supreme Court has upheld women's exemption because female soldiers are not ordered into direct ground combat. If the rules change, deliberately or by default, the ACLU will probably win. Voters will notice when their daughters are denied college loans for not registering with Selective Service.

President Bush, the ultimate "decider," should pay attention and intervene.

Physical Obstacles to Women in Combat

In the combat arms, physical capabilities are critical. Soldiers routinely carry weapons and equipment weighing 100 pounds or more. Servicewomen experience stress fractures and other injuries at rates far higher than men, but Army leaders pretend that male and female warriors are virtually interchangeable. Gender-normed training standards, which never would be used when choosing football players for the Army/Navy game, contribute to the illusion of a "gender-free" Army.

Officials also pretend that sexual entanglements can be perfectly managed. But sexual misconduct in the forced intimacy of the combat arms, on either end of the "hostile/romantic" behavior spectrum, would more seriously affect discipline and deployability, cohesion, and trust. No one should be surprised when demoralizing scandals similar to Abu Ghraib inspire more criticism of the military.

All soldiers—male and female—deserve our pride and support. They are not responsible for military leaders who disregard policy and law, but the Secretary of Defense is. President Bush, the ultimate "decider," should pay attention and intervene. Events in Iraq are beyond the president's control, but the Pentagon is not.

8

The Combat Exclusion Law Limits Women's Military Careers

Christopher T. Fulton

Lieutenant Colonel Christopher T. Fulton is the chief of staff of the Joint Functional Component Command—Global Strike and Integration at Offutt Air Force Base in Omaha, NE.

Although the U.S. Army allows women in most positions, it does not allow women officers to serve in the field artillery below the brigade level because of the ban on women in combat. Women officers who want to advance their careers in the field artillery are thwarted because they must serve at least two years as a battalion operations officers or executive officers and there are very few of these positions available. The Army, therefore, commissions women officers, but does not offer them competitive career paths, a practice that is prejudicial and limiting to women in the Army.

0620 Hours, 24 February; Iraqi Desert

Lead elements of the division have penetrated the initial obstacle belt of the defending Iraqis with minimal casualties. Iraqi soldiers surrender in droves and battle positions and armored vehicles lie destroyed or abandoned across the battlefield.

The secondary obstacle belt located 20 kilometers beyond is another matter. Not unlike the first layer of obstacles, this

Christopher T. Fulton, *Field Artillery (Wo)Men: Time for a Relook?*, U.S. Army War College, Defense Technical Information Center, April 7, 2003, pp. 1–15. www.dtic.mil.

belt is composed of continuous minefields 100 to 200 meters wide, with barbed wire, antitank ditches, berms, and oil filled trenches. This will require the division's soldiers to conduct a significant breach under direct and indirect enemy fire—and now in daylight. Combat engineers move into position, but are pinned down immediately and begin taking heavy casualties. Cpt [Captain] Mary Smith from the chemical company leads the company smoke vehicles forward to lay down a thick haze to mask the engineer team's efforts. Two of Cpt Smith's vehicles take direct hits from fortified enemy tank positions. A radio call goes back to the command post; progress is slow and casualties are mounting. Meanwhile, a platoon of Kiowa and Apache helicopters arrive, commanded by Cpt Susan Jones. 1LT [First Lieutenant] Diana White scouts forward in a Kiowa to locate the fortified enemy positions and relays the location to Captain Jones who then moves forward and directs engagement of the tanks with hellfire missiles.

Suddenly, emergency radio traffic—a Scud missile is tracking toward the vicinity of the breaching effort. Soldiers in the breeching site scramble for cover—and for their chemical protective masks—while another unit commanded by Colonel Heidi Brown scrambles to action. Soon two plumes from Patriot missiles are observed in the distance, successfully destroying the Scud. The significant signature of the Patriot launch gets the attention of forward deployed Iraqi operatives who initiate a ground assault on the Patriot position. Col Brown's soldiers engage the enemy and succeed in driving the attackers from their site—but at a cost of multiple casualties. At the same time, additional plumes are observed as Cpt Michele Ray's MLRS [Multiple Launch Rocket System] unit engages the Scud launch site with two ATACMS [Army Tactical Missile Systems] missiles.

The engineering effort continues to make progress. 1LT Sarah Williams personally leads the Fox chemical vehicle to the breaching site to conduct chemical sampling. Although significantly degraded, enemy resistance continues and one of the Fox vehicles is destroyed, killing all crewmembers.

Following 55 minutes of close combat in one of the toughest scenarios the engineers could have imagined, the breech is complete and initial armored vehicles move through the obstacle and deploy to destroy the remnants of the Iraqi resistance. On to Baghdad. . . .

[T]he Army is commissioning female field artillery officers . . . without providing them a viable, or competitive future.

This scenario did not play out on the Arabian Peninsula in 1991. In fact, it could not have. The reason for this has nothing to do with the type of battle being waged; U.S forces did deal with significant obstacle belts just as onerous as those described. What differ in this scenario are the players. Captains Smith, Jones, and Ray, Lieutenants White and Williams, and Colonel Brown would not have been serving in the positions described in 1991. U.S. law said they could not. All are women.

Women and the Field Artillery

Fast-forward to 2003 and a similar scenario. Every women listed could, and real women do, serve in the positions described—except one. Cpt "Michele" Ray would have to be named "Michael" Ray; the Field Artillery still does not allow women officers to serve in units below the brigade level.

This paper will examine the role of field artillery "women"—their past contributions, their present predicament—and recommend revisiting the 1999 Army decision denying assignment of female officers to MLRS.

This paper is not a plea of passion to open the gates of all field artillery units or all combat arms to women. Nor is it about the expansion of the field artillery to enlisted women, although the case presented may provide insights valuable to that issue. This paper is specifically about the present Army policy of commissioning women into the officer ranks of the field artillery.

Simply stated, the Army is commissioning female field artillery officers, albeit in small numbers, without providing them a viable, or competitive, future. This does not need to be the case. It is now possible to create a career path that not only meets current law, but also provides expanded opportunities for qualified women officers wanting to serve their country in the field artillery. . . .

Operation Desert Storm significantly impacted American perceptions of women in combat, so much so that in 1994 the Secretary of Defense rescinded the Risk Rule and instead established a new DOD [Department of Defense] wide direct ground combat assignment rule allowing service members to be assigned to all positions for which they qualified. The intent of this change was to expand opportunities for women in light of the probability of theater-wide risk such as that found in Desert Storm. The exception remained excluding women from assignment to units below the brigade level whose primary mission was direct ground combat.

What did those changes mean for the assignment of women in the field artillery? Inexplicitly, the simple answer is "not much." Although combat aviation, naval vessels and some elements of Army ground forces such as air defense and other combat support and combat service support branches were affected by these changes, the field artillery, still considered a combat arm, remains closed to women in tactical units below the brigade level. . . .

Limited Opportunities for Women

The true challenge for women lies at the field-grade level and the requirement for field artillery officers to complete two years in a branch-qualifying position. This means a major must serve at least two years as a battalion Operations Officer

61

or Executive Officer. Notice the level must be "battalion." The only battalion-level positions available to female field artillery officers are as Executive Officers in the Field Artillery Training Center as well as a select few TDA [Table of Distribution and Allowances, non-combat] positions also at Fort Sill and a sprinkling of positions throughout the garrison Army. Because of these limited opportunities, field grade women in the field artillery are significantly disadvantaged compared to their male counterparts.

Can they make it despite this obstacle? Thankfully the answer is yes. However, the quality of women leader required for success under this path far outweighs the quality required to make it through the tactical route. That is truly a strong statement, but if success is measured by selection for command at the battalion level, only two women have made that mark to date.

Why are women allowed to request the field artillery . . . if no enhancing opportunities are provided for their advancement commensurate with their male peers?

Given that lack of opportunity, the first logical question one might pose is this: Why would a woman even consider the field artillery as a career field? The simple answer—she can! U.S. Army regulations still allow women officers to request positioning in the field artillery, or as stated in U.S. Army Regulation 600–13, "to serve in any officer . . . position except in those specialties, positions, or units (battalion size or smaller) which are assigned the routine mission to engage in direct combat, or which collocate routinely with units assigned a direct combat mission." This *official* position clearly allows women to request commissioning in the field artillery—with limitations to the type unit she can serve in. . . .

No Viable Career Path for Women in Field Artillery

Given *she can*, a woman requesting assignment to the field artillery branch is made fully aware of the consequences of her action. Specifically, every women requesting field artillery as a branch choice must be counseled by the Reserve Officer Training Corps (ROTC) Professor of Military Science (or United States Military Academy equivalent) utilizing the Standardized Briefing for Women Considering Field Artillery, which states: "It is in your best interest to think through very carefully your decision to request the Field Artillery Branch. Though the branch is open to women, there are constraints that must be considered before making your final branch decision."

[F]emale officers commissioned into the field artillery have a future limited in both scope and responsibility.

So she can, but should she? The answer to that question is also simple—it simply doesn't matter. Regardless of their personal motivations, desires, or ambitions, women are among the ranks of the field artillery and Army policy allows them to be there. The better questions to ask would be to the Army. Why are women allowed to request the field artillery as a basic branch if no enhancing career opportunities are provided for their advancement commensurate with their male peers? More importantly, what is the Army—and specifically the Commanders of Major Army Commands (MACOMs)—doing to meet their regulatory requirement to "ensure that the assignment of women provides full career opportunities to reach their highest potential." The answer is again simple—they aren't. The Army is commissioning women into the ranks of the field artillery and not providing them a competitive, viable career path—contrary to regulation and often masked in issues that are irrelevant given the changing nature of modern combat. . . .

The Army Must Provide
Career Paths for Women

Successful integration of women into our armed forces will continue to generate animosity in certain circles no matter the argument provided. But the simple fact is that the momentum of this integration appears to be picking up steam; the recent air defense expansion of positions for women is one example.

Yet unlike the air defense, female officers commissioned into the field artillery have a future limited in both scope and responsibility. Their assignment limitations to levels of brigade or above, or more significantly and problematically to TDA [Table of Distribution and Allowances] units exclusively, is a detriment to their competitiveness with their male peers assigned to tactical units. If this were not the case, the counseling statement a woman must sign when applying for commissioning in field artillery would not have the warning: "The lack of a weapon system opportunity in the early years of an officer's career may be a discriminator."

Now is the time to either accept women into an expanded role in positions within the field artillery where they can successfully serve and contribute, or cease the unfair and prejudicial practice of commissioning women into the field artillery in the first place. Stopping the commissioning of women is *not* required or appropriate. What is required is for the Army to provide a successful and meaningful career path within the field artillery for women already commissioned in the branch, and those who wish to be commissioned in the branch.

9

The Combat Exclusion Law Does Not Limit Women in the Military

Ellen Embrey

Ellen Embrey is the deputy assistant secretary of defense for Force Health Protection and Readiness.

Women have traditionally served the United States in the military. Beginning in 1974, women have been able to fill jobs previously only held by men and enjoy the same promotions and benefits as men. Since 1993, many additional combat assignments have been available to women in the Air Force and Navy. Women in the Army are also filling important roles on the battlefield. Consequently, women are able to fulfill their career goals in the military, despite the combat exclusion rule.

In this special month set aside to honor women's history, we need to look to our past to see clearly into our future. Our strength and our resolve come from a rich heritage, so it is appropriate that we reflect on the accomplishments of the past to see where the future may lead.

In particular, it is the women who have served our country in the military who have had a major impact in setting the course for the women of today and tomorrow. It is most appropriate today for us to remember what they did, and to recognize their deeds. . . .

Ellen Embrey, "Military Women Pioneering the Future," *Deployment Link*, March 28, 2003. Reproduced by permission.

A Changed Military

[I]n June 1973, the entire military was significantly changed. No longer conscripted, the military became an all-volunteer force. While this was a new concept for men, it wasn't for women who served—they all had been volunteers from the outset. With this change, the number of women in service began to grow. In 1974, Army women were assigned into branches previously occupied by men, except for Infantry, Armor and Field Artillery. And they were now promoted equally with their men counterparts. And the role continued to change.

In 1975, by public law, women began to pioneer another new frontier—the service academies. The following year, in 1976—200 years after Molly Pitcher, Sarah Fulton and Margaret Corbin [women who served in the American Revolution] had served in the military—119 women were the first to enter the U.S. Military Academy at West Point; 81 entered the U.S. Naval Academy at Annapolis; and 157 entered the U.S. Air Force Academy in Colorado Springs. Before they graduated in 1980, a separate corps for them was no longer needed. In the Army, women had been assimilated effectively in training assignments, logistics and administrative management. Members of the Women's Army Corps, both officers and enlisted, had grown in number—from about 16,000, in 1972, to 56,841, by September 30, 1978. Then, on October 20, 1978, the Women's Army Corps was disestablished. The other services followed similar paths. Military women now trained and served at locations throughout the world—serving not as WACs, WAVEs and WAFs [women's branches of the Army, Navy and Airforce], but as soldiers, sailors, airmen, Marines and Coast Guardsmen. Side by side, as members of a well-trained team, they served with their men counterparts.

Those who had doubted their capabilities were pleasantly surprised. This evolution went largely unnoticed until October 1983, during Operation Urgent Fury. Women MPs [Military

Police] from Fort Bragg deployed with their units to Grenada. Upon reaching their destination, however, they were recalled to the United States; then, three days later, they returned. Their commander said the initial decision to withdraw them wasn't the right one. "If there's a battle," he said, "the women will stay and complete their mission."

Six years later, in 1989, the question of whether women should serve with their units wasn't even asked. Before the invasion of Panama, 620 women were already stationed there, and 170 more were sent. They continued the proud tradition of those who'd gone before them. And we remember.

Women Served in the First Gulf War

Who then could have imagined that a year later this all-volunteer force, composed of men and women, would face its first large-scale challenge [the First Gulf War]? This force was, for the most part, untested. Could they do the job? Would their equipment work? Could they withstand the harsh environment a continent away? News magazines, cover after cover, examined the all-volunteer force and placed special scrutiny on the women, then nearly 11 percent of the entire force on active duty. Not only did women withstand the microscopic scrutiny, they served professionally and withstood the blistering heat of summer and the cold, windy, dust-filled desert winters. They were there to deter war by being ready to wage it. And when Saddam Hussein [former dictator of Iraq] failed to comply with the United Nations deadline, they, with their units—their comrades—crossed the line in the sand. About 3,800 Air Force women, in units of both the active and reserve components, served in the desert. When the air campaign began, they were there—serving in military airlift, airlift terminal and cargo management, aerial refueling, communications, intelligence, fire fighting, aeromedical evacuation and a wide variety of support specialties. Women Air Force pilots flew and crewed strategic transports, tactical transports, tankers, reconnaissance and aeromedical airlift aircraft. When the ground war began, 26,000 Army women and 1,000 women Marines were there with their units. They served in a wide variety of specialties, including military police, intelligence, communications and civil affairs. They flew helicopters, drove trucks and operated the Patriot missiles. One thousand Navy women were part of the campaign, as well. They served on hospital ships, supply ships, repair ships, oilers and ammunition ships. They flew helicopters and reconnaissance aircraft and served in Navy construction battalions. In all, nearly 35,000 women served. Fifteen of them died; four of them, all enlisted soldiers, were killed in action. Two women, an Army truck driver and an Army flight surgeon, were taken prisoner. But this you know. You saw them on television, in magazines and newspapers. You welcomed them home, and you mourned with those families whose sons and daughters, husbands and wives, fathers and mothers made the supreme sacrifice for our country. To all of them, you were then a grateful nation. You recognized their professional commitment and patriotism. By your actions you thanked them. You remembered.

[M]ilitary women today are moving out to openly explore the forward frontier of the combat zone more fully than ever.

New Assignments Are Opened for Women

A historic change in assignment policy occurred in 1993 when combat aviation specialties and assignments on Navy combat ships were opened to women. Then-Secretary of Defense Les Aspin explained the change. He said: "We know from experience that women can fly our high-performance fighter aircraft. We know from experience that they can perform well in assignments at sea. And we know from Operations Desert Storm and Desert Shield that women can stand up to the most demanding environments."

Between the first Gulf War and today [March 2003], military women continued to push the boundaries, pioneering new frontiers. According to the Defense Manpower Data Center, more than 1,000 women participated in U.S. military operations in Somalia between 1992 and 1994.

In 1995 more than 1,200 women were deployed to Haiti for peacekeeping duties.

To date, more than 5,000 women have served in the peacekeeping operations in Bosnia.

And less than two months ago [January 2003], military women pioneered previously uncharted area on a mission in the skies over Afghanistan. On Jan. 31 [2003], a KC-135 Stratotanker took off from Ganci Air Base, Kyrgyzstan, carrying more than 180,000 pounds of fuel. It was also carrying the first all-female crew to fly an air refueling mission into Afghanistan from Ganci. I can't give you their names, for reasons of operational security, but the two pilots, navigator, and boom operator have been deployed there from the 99th Air Refueling Squadron since Dec. 9 [2002]. Between the four of them, they have almost 4,000 flying hours in the KC-135, in places like Saudi Arabia, Qatar, Iceland and Thailand. They are just four of the 1,800 women supporting Operation Enduring Freedom.

Today the legacy of these soldiers, sailors, airmen, Marines and Coast Guardsmen lives on. Their proud tradition doesn't end here. It lives on.

The only thing stopping you is you. . . . There's no goal that you can't reach.

U.S. law does still bar women from ground combat. Nonetheless, military women today are moving out to openly explore the forward frontier of the combat zone more fully than ever.

Women Reach Their Career Goals

In the *Christian Science Monitor* I read about Specialist Danielle Barnaba who drives a five-ton delivery truck out in the desert, hauling everything from engine parts to toothpaste on her daily supply runs to Army combat brigades. She's one of the soldiers of the 703rd Main Support Battalion, which runs the lifeline for the Third Infantry Division and at 26, she's driving a 10-wheeler that might be older than she is.

The *Washington Post* wrote about Army chief warrant officer Charisma Henzie, who spent her 26th birthday on the current deployment. Henzie flies CH-47 Chinook helicopters the big haulers that look like green school buses with rotors front and back. Chinooks are cargo and troop helicopters that often fly to front-line positions. Machinegunners ride on both sides and at the tail. Right now she might be ferrying soldiers into battle, dropping reconnaissance teams behind enemy lines or zipping into Iraqi territory to refuel Apache attack helicopters.

Warrant Officer Laquitta Joseph was featured in the *Wall Street Journal*. Ms. Joseph is responsible for making sure the equipment works in her unit—the 317th engineering battalion of the third brigade combat team of the Army's Third Infantry Division. And when combat engineers say "equipment" they mean minefield-clearing machines, 14-ton bridge-building contraptions and armored personnel carriers. She's traveling right behind those front-line combat engineers who clear minefields and build, or blow up, bridges. In a sense, that makes Ms. Joseph one of the most "forward" women in the Iraqi Theater. Because when something breaks down she goes to the front line to find the problem and figure out how to fix it.

I also want to mention Chief Warrant Officer 4 Concetta Hassan, the Chinook helicopter pilot with B Company, 159th Aviation Regiment. She's the 60-year-old grandmother that *USA Today* wrote about a few days ago [March 2003]. Ms.

Hassan has served her country in uniform since 1975. Six years into her Army career, she applied for flight school and made it. She flew in Honduras, she flew in Korea, and now she's flying in current operations for Central Command.

[P]atriotic, selfless service . . . knows no gender.

She says that when women join the military, this is what she tries to impart to them. "The only thing stopping you is you. . . . There's no goal that you can't reach."

I don't want you to think that the only fighting women today are wearing Army green. A recent story in the *Washington Post* reported that even now, years after the first woman joined the crew of the *USS Abraham Lincoln*, women are gaining in numbers but are still very much a minority in a male-dominated environment. For example, when the ship store got a rare box of small Hanes T-shirts, women snapped them up. And women's restrooms on the ship are hard to find. The *Lincoln* is one of the Navy's largest aircraft carriers, so even though women make up only about 10 percent of her crew, that still means more than 500 female sailors going into harm's way with their male counterparts.

The Future for Military Women

Well, that's the state of military women in the past and in the present. Where will the future lead? Perhaps the future female pioneers will be led by women like Air Force Lieutenant Colonel Eileen Collins. She's the pilot who was named the first female space shuttle commander. According to NASA, Lt. Col. Collins is one of 27 women out of 229 people who have flown in the history of the space shuttle program. Collins became the first woman to pilot a space shuttle when she flew aboard a mission in February 1995—the first flight of the new joint Russian-American space program.

Pioneering military women have pushed the boundaries since this country was formed, continually revising the role of women in our society. What do those serving think of these changes? Says one Army aviator, "I knew it would happen—not by revolution, but by evolution." Says another: "I am pleased with these changes, and I'm proud of those who served so well before I joined. But more than anything, I want to be regarded not as a woman soldier, but as a soldier." A soldier first, because the patriotic, selfless service—of those who served before, those who now serve, and those who will serve in the future—knows no gender. When we think of those soldiers, sailors, airmen, Marines, and Coast Guardsmen, we must remember the young women who dedicate their time, talents and—yes, their very lives—to protecting our nation. By doing so, they are pioneering the path to the future. And we will remember.

10

Women in Combat Roles Weaken the U.S. Armed Services

George Neumayr

George Neumayr is the managing editor of American Spectator *magazine.*

The death of women in Iraq can be attributed to a feminist push for women soldiers to be assigned to combat roles in order to advance their military careers. Although there is a ban on women in land combat units, the Army has positioned women in support roles near the front lines to satisfy feminist demands. Female presence in combat units weakens the combat readiness of the troops because women cannot physically handle the demands of combat, and men feel the need to protect them at the cost of their own safety.

The casualty lists from the Middle East contain a sick progress report on feminism in the U.S. military. Mothers sent into the war on terrorism are coming home to their children in body bags. Among the war dead: Lori Ann Piestewa, 23, mother of two preschoolers; Melissa J. Hobart, 22, mother of a 3-year-old; Jessica L. Cawvey, 21, single mother of a 6-year-old; Pamela Osbourne, 38, mother of three children, ages 9–19; Katrina L. Bell-Johnson, 32, mother of a 1-year-old.

George Bush's military isn't reconsidering the feminist experiment devised under Bill Clinton; it is completing it. The

George Neumayr, "Your Mother's Army," *American Spectator*, vol. 38, no. 4, May 2005, pp. 24–27. www.spectator.org.

Army increasingly relies on women even as it lethargically and ineffectually recruits men. (The Army missed its recruiting goal in February [2005] by 27 percent.) Women now constitute 15 percent of the active Army, 23 percent of the Army Reserve, and 13 percent of the Army National Guard. It is commonly estimated that 30 percent of the Army will be female by 2010.

More Women Are on the Battlefield

Claudia Kennedy, a general under Bill Clinton who entered the military after filling out an Army enlistment coupon she found in *Cosmopolitan* magazine and is credited with launching the Army's "Consideration of Others" program, once said to West Point cadets, "This is not your father's Army anymore!" Her boast is even truer under Bush's Pentagon, which has been pushing more and more women onto the battlefield, forming the beginnings of a coed front line. As of this spring [2005], roughly 17,000 female soldiers had been in Iraq and Afghanistan, serving in de facto combat roles even though their positions are technically described as "support."

In February [2005], even as the Army insisted that it wasn't abolishing the prohibition on women in ground combat units, its 3rd Infantry Division confirmed that it was placing women side by side with combat troops in "forward support" positions, a policy called "collocation." The Army cited as its reason for the new policy a shortage of qualified men. But Elaine Donnelly of the Center for Military Readiness was told by Pentagon officials that "this is how women grow their careers." (A military source who e-mailed *TAS* [*The American Spectator* magazine] also pinpointed feminist careerism as the real reason for the change, writing, "All of this is entirely for the purpose of ensuring that women in the military have the opportunity to become generals, even though the only real purpose of having generals at all is for the leading of military units in actual combat and making and deciding on overall strategic considerations as they pertain to the impending battles.")

Given the choice between feminism and maximum military effectiveness, the Army is choosing feminism.

When the policy drew fire from critics like Donnelly (who established that it skirted the law and that the Army has been secretly tinkering with gender codes for units in an unclassified document titled "Combat Exclusion Quick Look Options"), the Army offered up the absurd sop of promising to evacuate the female troops should these collocated units run into battle conditions—an outrageously convoluted plan which only underscored the Army's willingness to juggle feminism at the expense of its essential military mission.

One soldier who heard about the new gender-integrated collocation policy described it as a formula for losing battles and getting soldiers killed, since evacuating female troops will mean dissipating crucial resources at the very moment these ground combat units will need them most. Assets, he said, "cannot be spared simply to move females to the rear. . . . Imagine an entire brigade trying to chopper out these female contingents before combat—it would require almost half of a division's worth of aviation assets to move them all at once."

The Army Chooses Feminism

Given the choice between feminism and maximum military effectiveness, the Army is choosing feminism. But as the Army nudges women to the frontlines and unfolds the feminist logic of equal rights requiring equal risks, the shocks of war are becoming more terrifyingly real to women, the majority of whom reveal in surveys that they have no desire to serve on the frontlines. Many female soldiers had an image of life in the military as careerism without combat—an image military recruiters eager to meet female quotas don't discourage.

"You're not generally told as a female that you will be in that type of situation where you are in harm's way directly," said National Guard Sergeant Brenda Monroe to the *Sacramento Bee*. "I never dreamed that I would wake up every night and have to run to a bunker and take cover because we were being attacked or under direct fire."

The rescued soldier Jessica Lynch makes a similar observation in her memoirs, noting that she never anticipated even being in a position to be raped and kidnapped by the enemy. After former Notre Dame basketball player Danielle Green had her left hand blown off during an attack in Iraq her old Irish coach Muffet McGraw said to reporters, "It was just a shock to hear she had been injured because she had said that her job was going to keep her on the sidelines."

War Is More Traumatic for Women

The first shock of war for female soldiers is that they are actually in it. But it is not the last one. A story that much of the media have ignored is that a significant number of female soldiers exposed to the traumas of war are returning from the Middle East with serious psychological problems. The *Sacramento Bee* to its credit reported in March that female soldiers are suffering a high incidence of post-traumatic stress disorder. "Returning female vets are bringing back wounded minds, beset by post-traumatic stress disorder, an illness that affects women at twice the rate of men." Military doctors fear an "avalanche of cases among female vets will smother the military health care system," it reported.

The *Bee* added that at the Veteran Affairs' Post-Traumatic Stress Disorder (PTSD) center in White River Junction, Vermont, researchers "are completing a $5 million study of 384 female vets with PTSD." Several studies are underway and doctors are reaching the obvious conclusion, that war is more traumatic for women than men.

Researchers, according to the *Bee*, "have found female brains may be less efficient than male brains at producing the neurosteroids that help human beings cope with stress. Other studies have shown women deplete serotonin, a substance that helps combat depression, more quickly than men and regenerate it more slowly. And menstrual cycles may also play a role in making women more vulnerable in stressful situations."

Since many of the mothers in the military are single . . . many luckless children are left with no parents.

Meanwhile, the Army itches to send even more women into crippling combat conditions, as ambitious generals glance anxiously over their shoulders at Hillary Clinton on the Armed Services Committee. (Stephanie Gutmann, author of *The Kinder, Gentler Military*, has reported that many in Congress have long demanded an Army composed of 50 percent women, and that the Army's recruiting philosophy of women is, "Get'em on the plane.") While George Bush has said "no women in combat," he acts as if the matter is out of his hands. "There's no change of policy as far as I'm concerned," he passively said to the *Washington Times* in January [2005].

In a "Message from the Army Leadership" earlier this year, its heads proudly related how "women are exposed to combat danger as they perform aviation missions, ground convoy security, united resupply operations, and a host of other critical functions." Nothing has given the Pentagon pause—not reports of eroding standards in training, not the Abu Ghraib debacle of women wardens and run-amok female jailers, not bodybags carrying the nation's mothers and daughters, not women soldiers tortured and held in captivity, not the growing list of orphans.

Separating Mothers from Toddlers Is Barbaric

The Army's blatantly barbaric policy of separating mothers from their toddlers is even a point of pride, cast as a principled refusal to surrender the feminist idea that men and women must carry the same responsibilities if they wish to enjoy the same benefits. (By contrast, in the Korean War, no woman with a child under 18 was permitted to serve.) Before separating children from their mothers, the Army issues to military moms ludicrous literature on "children and deployment" (one of the accompanying pictures is of a woman cradling an infant) in which books on "Family-Change Situations" are extolled, such as "All Kinds of Families" and "The Good-bye Painting."

"The child may become confused and fearful that Mommy or Daddy will abandon them," the Army counsels, and suggests female troops leave behind a laminated photo of the themselves: "the 'I want my daddy/mommy syndrome' can be helped by supplying the child with a laminated photo. . . ." The Army also suggests that "children record cassettes to the soldier. This is good for toddlers who are learning how to talk; it keeps the soldier in touch with their progress." (It is not uncommon for mothers still nursing their children to be deployed. Since many of the mothers in the military are single mothers—women in the military are twice as likely as men to be single parents—many luckless children are left with no parents.)

Why the Army is fostering this dysfunctional mess, so surreal it seems like a Sci-Fi movie or an Aristophanes play, and deliberately makes itself dependent on those least capable of winning wars, is a source of mystery and bitterness to many male soldiers.

In a letter to *TAS* one soldier wrote that the Army is rapidly squandering its strength for the sake of placing women in roles they obviously can't fill. "I am constantly amazed at how little actual time [female soldiers] have spent in the field, how little combat training they have, and how mentally soft most of them are," he wrote. He recalled his training in a Marine Reserve unit which had women: "The women generally stayed at the drill hall when we went to the field. During one training cycle, however, some of the women participated in an urban warfare course. One of them promptly broke her leg doing a spider drop out a window. Her smaller frame could not take the shock of landing after dropping 6 feet or so while weighed down with all the equipment a Marine is expected to wear in battle. . . . I sincerely hope the Army will step back and evaluate how dumbing down training for the purposes of political correctness is not the way to win wars."

[T]he Army frequently finds itself spending as much energy doing damage control over sexual impropriety as it does to fight battles.

Women Damage the Military

In another letter shared with *TAS*, an infantry officer writes that feminizing the military has damaged training standards before war (so men are entering war less prepared), undermined the effectiveness of units during war (as men confusedly compensate for a chaotic division of labor in which they must do their jobs and the jobs of unqualified women too, such as helping women not strong enough change the tires of the trucks they are assigned to drive), and caused morale-sapping sexual tension and scandal, a problem that has become an enormous distraction.

He writes: "Most fighting men will admit that combat readiness suffers with women, who overwhelmingly cannot be counted on as equals. This is due to a physical inability to complete some of the most basic of soldier tasks, such as carrying a full load of equipment plus weapon, changing truck tires, breaking track or carrying a wounded man."

He was "astonished to discover that the first infantry battalion I was assigned to in the 4th Infantry Division in 2003 depended on a 'forward support company' comprised of a significant number of female soldiers." His "infantry battalion had to send six women from its support company home from Iraq due to pregnancy. No one wanted to talk about or admit this; it would not have been politically correct to note the rampant sexual promiscuity among both the single and the married soldiers within the all male infantry battalion and the two dozen or so women in the support company."

Later serving in another division, he witnessed the same disruptive effects of women in combat: "Enlisted troops participated in orgies in secluded areas while senior enlisted and even officers were all too willing to lose their composure over female subordinates. In brigade and division headquarters areas, sexual discipline was a joke with commanders preferring instead to rely on the local medics to hand out prophylactics while ignoring what was going on . . . the Army frequently finds itself spending as much energy doing damage control over sexual impropriety as it does to fight battles. I have seen entire headquarters paralyzed from gender-related tensions."

Male soldiers are officially trained not to behave chivalrously toward women soldiers, to accept with indifference that women like Jessica Lynch will be raped and tortured, to work in coed units where women, as the *Sacramento Bee* puts it, urinate in the open and are told to "shed any qualms about cleaning yourself up in front of men." Is it surprising that out of this raw and coarse culture in the military came the squalid hijinks of Abu Ghraib [a prisoner of war jail where U.S. soldiers mistreated Iraqi prisoners in 2003 and 2004] and now reports of frequent sexual harassment and assault? The Defense Department has had to disclose embarrassingly that one out of seven women at its military academies say they have been sexually assaulted.

How high will the costs of feminism in the military have to climb before Bush's Pentagon admits that its feminist dream is more like a nightmare?

11

Banning Women from Combat Is Ethically Wrong

Erin Solaro

Erin Solaro is the author of the book Women in the Line of Fire: What You Should Know about Women in the Military, *published in 2006.*

Women are serving in the military, but none of the disasters predicted by opponents of women in the military has come to pass. Although subject to a ban on women in combat, female soldiers often engage in warfare. Consequently, the combat exclusion rule is immoral because it denies women combat training and puts them in more danger rather than less. In addition, the combat exclusion rule is unethical because it stigmatizes women, encourages men to think of them as incompetent in combat, and denies women the full rights and duties of citizenship.

My name is Erin Solaro. Thank you for inviting me [to speak at the U.S. Military Academy] and thank you for being here.

I'm the author of *Women in the Line of Fire*, to my knowledge the first book to seriously address the experiences of the more than 165,000 women who have deployed to Afghanistan and Iraq since 9/11. I'm here to talk about the issues these women and their experiences raise for you as cadets and future officers of a military going where no military has gone

Erin Solaro, "The Woman Soldier: Biology, Equality, and the Common Defense," Speech given at the U.S. Military Academy for the Margaret Corbin Forum, March 27, 2007. www.erinsolaroandphilipgold.wordpress.com. Reproduced by permission.

before. That is the open integration of relatively large numbers of women in combat units as volunteer professionals. . . .

I plan to address three major issues.

First: What I saw in Iraq in 2004 and Afghanistan in 2005 and all the disasters that haven't happened where women are concerned.

Second: What the military needs to do to complete the process of achieving women's full equality under arms, both at unit level and institutionally.

Third: Why women's full equality under arms is a good thing. . . .

Women Soldiers in Iraq and Afghanistan

The first is what I saw in Iraq, where I was embedded with the Army's First Brigade Combat Team, First Infantry Division, at Camp Junction City in Anbar Province and 2/4 Marines in Ramadi, as well as in Afghanistan, where I worked out of Bagram Air Field and was embedded with combat troops and with Parwan and Ghanzi Provincial Reconstruction Teams.

As I mentioned, over 165,000 American servicewomen have gone to war as volunteer professionals. Women are now 15% of the military, 11% of the deployed troops and an unprecedented 2% of the casualties. Perhaps the most striking aspect of this is what hasn't happened: none of the disasters so gleefully predicted by opponents of women in the military and of women's equality generally. No significant combat failures due to the presence of women. No epidemics of rape or what I call "get me out of here" pregnancies. No massive breakdowns in discipline, no orgies 24/7. Where bad things have occurred—and there are still some monstrous things—they generally happen in units that have larger and more fundamental problems of leadership and discipline. Every unit has its ten percent of jerks and worse. In good units, they don't dare get out of line; if they do, they're dealt with quickly and firmly. In bad units, they set the tone. In such units, women suffer, and are suffering now. But the solution is not to remove or punish women for the crimes and failures of others. The solution is to nail the perps and their active and passive accessories and collaborators.

[W]omen are going out with small infantry and special operations units from which they are still legally barred.

I am not saying there have been no significant problems, nor many small problems. Nor am I claiming there never will be, especially given the operational and personnel pressures on the Army and Marines. But if really disastrous things had happened, believe me, they'd have been leaked. And let me add here, regarding the unsubstantiated accusations from anonymous sources that people like Elaine Donnelly [president of the Center for Military Readiness] publicize, unnamed units and individuals don't count. As with tales regarding war crimes, those who tell such stories and those who pass them on, have an absolute obligation to have the facts and be ready to share the facts. Nor does "It would end my career to speak out" mean anything, if you're a person in uniform. Courage is courage. And lies are lies.

So what has happened? We now have women in combat routinely. Sometimes combat comes to them, in the course of their other duties. But more and more, women are going out with small infantry and special operations units from which they are still legally barred. In Iraq and Afghanistan I went on raids and patrols with women who were there to search and handle Iraqi and Afghan women and children, but who were expected to fight if necessary, and who did. In Afghanistan, I interviewed women who'd done long missions with Navy SEALs and Army Special Forces. Women are now earning medals and combat ribbons and badges, including Sgt. Leigh Anne Hester, who won the first Silver Star awarded to a woman since World War II.

A New Generation of Soldiers

Even more importantly, in Iraq and Afghanistan I saw a new generation of soldiers, accustomed to equality since birth, making up the rules as they went along and making it work. I found that what you lose in privacy, you gain in modesty. I found that men and women with marriages or serious relationships back home would band together in "misery loves company" affinity groups to keep each other faithful. I found male soldiers quietly guarding the women in their units against outside predators. I found the men accepting the women on the only basis that really matters among soldiers: Can you trust this person to carry her share of the load? Most of all, can you trust her when, as it was known in past wars, it's time to "enter the world of hurt."

For a man to intentionally harm his [soldier] sisters is a profoundly shameful act that should be regarded as such. . . .

More and more, they can. Equality works, not least of all because men and women want more from each other than sex. And I say this without trivializing the observation of a female captain and combat veteran, now a civilian wife working with military families, who wrote in a recent email: "The silent morale killer is knowing you can have liaisons if you want them. But marriage, a family, a life partner, children? With this operational tempo and, currently, no end in sight?"

To institutionalize the reality of women's performance, the military needs to ask Congress to repeal the combat exclusion law and drop all remaining restrictions on women's combat service. We know, or at least can be reasonably certain, that there will come a time when the military and the American people find themselves going through another national debate about women in the military, their place and their roles. It is time the military got out in front of that debate. . . .

And the task for every man who knows that the time is over when women had to regard harassment and assault as the price of wearing the uniform—and who wants to make sure that day never, ever returns—is to back those "sensitivity trainers" up, morally and legally, formally and informally.

To put it a bit differently: Despite all the rules and regulations, the military is essentially a shame society, not a guilt society. Reputation, honor and respect are everything. For a man to intentionally harm his sisters is a profoundly shameful act that should be regarded as such—and he should be treated accordingly.

[T]he exclusion stigmatizes servicewomen as second class and untrustworthy in a fight.

Finally, over the last decades, we have seen a phenomenon that can only be described as "fragging by rape"—the use of sexual harassment and assault to drive women out of a unit or a service. No one who does, abets or tolerates this is fit to wear the uniform, let alone serve as an officer.

That said, your responsibility as officers requires more than enforcing civility and the respect soldiers owe each other. You have an obligation to insist people make sense of this database that we now have of professional servicewomen's performance on deployment and in combat—including Combat Action Badges and Ribbons, Bronze Stars with "V," and the Silver Star. Including all the soldierly deeds that don't win medals. And yes, including the physical and psychological price women now pay to win those medals and do those deeds. . . .

To Exclude Women
from Combat Is Immoral

Combat is the core of the profession of arms, and exposure to combat an inherent risk of that profession. Thus the military has an absolute right to expect servicewomen to engage in combat, whether they are combat troops or not. Instead, the military continues, in the face of reality, to maintain the institutional pretense that women will not really have to engage in involuntary combat, while refusing to even let women volunteer for combat positions.

This was—and is—immoral.

I know many men do not choose combat positions: from the overwhelming majority of men in the Air Force to a small majority in the Marine Corps. Nevertheless, for those men, it is a choice that stigmatizes neither them as individuals nor their sex as a group who cannot be counted upon in combat.

The combat exclusion policy—now law, and only partially ameliorated by the opening of naval and aviation combat positions to women—has two pernicious results. First, the exclusion stigmatizes servicewomen as second class and untrustworthy in a fight. This stigma means the good men can't trust them and leaves them endlessly vulnerable to disrespect, harassment, and assault by dirtbags and criminals. Second, the law also makes servicewomen far more vulnerable to the enemy's attention than the enemy is to theirs. This is not a result of today's non-linear battlefield. In the early 80s, when we were still planning to fight the Soviets in Cold War Europe, servicewomen were clustered in high-value targets such as intelligence units, headquarters, and logistics depots. Anyone who understood Soviet doctrine knew that if the Cold War went hot, servicewomen would die in numbers all out of proportion to their presence in the military. When the military said women were in non-combat positions, they meant that women were excluded from learning how to fight and being able to kill, not from being killed.

Obviously, the military owes no individual any specific position and it cannot promise anyone that they will come home alive. What the military owes to everyone in service is candor about their risks and training that prepares them mentally and physically for those risks, that they may prevail against the enemy.

It is profoundly immoral to force women, because they are women, to be more vulnerable to the enemy than the enemy is to them—much less lie about that reality to them.

And now a final truth.

By now, we know that all pretense aside, the military is increasingly counting upon women to engage in ground combat. At the same time, the military is also institutionally unwilling to go before Congress and the public to say, "You should allow us to admit our sisters to the profession of arms as our equals by dropping all combat restrictions. They have earned their equality, and it is wrong to withhold from them their just due."

It is profoundly dishonorable for the military to increasingly rely upon women's willingness to engage and perform in combat, while refusing to acknowledge that they are—and as military personnel should be—engaging in combat, and so deserve human and professional equality. . . .

Why Women in Combat Is Good for the Society

I would like, now, to conclude by discussing why the participation of women in combat as volunteer professionals is good for society, regardless of the outcome of the present wars.

Earlier, I mentioned, very briefly, maternal mortality without elaborating on it. Now, I am going to do so.

In modern Afghanistan, about 1 woman in 6 dies in childbirth—when you consider that not all Afghan women become pregnant, the real number amongst child-bearing women may be closer to 1 in 5—and more die of delayed complications.

Statistically, a US infantryman had a better chance of surviving World War Two. Afghanistan's statistics are probably close to the pre-20th century human norm, a norm that profoundly shaped relationships: between men and women, between men, between women, between us and our bodies, between us and the bodies of the other sex. More recently, between 1900 and 1960 alone, I estimate over 840,000 American women died in childbirth, a number that does not include deaths due to delayed complications. By comparison, only about 603,000 Americans, virtually all male, died in combat in major American wars from the Revolution to Korea; include all non-battle deaths and the war total rises to about 1.08 million.

Death in war, then, was an episodic horror; death in childbirth was a constant slaughter of women in what should have been their best years.

Men have no comparable physical vulnerability.

The formal, acknowledged participation of American women in combat . . . will mark the near completion of women's transition from chattel to citizen.

Not until about 1960 do we see children beginning to be borne by (very young) women whose own mothers had a good chance of surviving their own reproductive careers. The senior military leadership who oversaw the beginning of women's integration into the military was the last generation of men to grow up with the mass death of women. Perhaps some had caused the deaths of their own mothers, or lost them to subsequent births, or saw their sisters die. They certainly grew up and married with the visceral knowledge that they might cause their wives' deaths in childbirth and that when their children married, their sons-in-law might well kill their own daughters, their own sons might kill their daughters-in-law.

On the one hand, this knowledge imposed a binding moral obligation upon them, that no woman should have to bear the twin risks of combat and childbirth. On the other hand, for the sake of their own sanity, they had to steeply devalue women as human beings, much less as citizens and as soldiers. In our culture, that devaluation usually took the form of an idealization and *imputation of weakness* utterly divorced from reality. In other cultures, it took—and takes—far more vicious forms.

This is how much of the world still lives. This is how most of the women of the world still live. Whatever you think of the war in Iraq, the Pentagon gets it right: this is going to be a very long war about the kind of world we will all live in. And the women of the developing world, if we take them seriously, could be our natural allies. In Iraq and Afghanistan, I watched them watch GI Jane, armed, modest, competent, accepted as an equal by her brothers. I could see in their eyes that they saw freedom.

I don't mean that they approve of us: I know some of them hate us. I don't mean that they suddenly want to be soldiers, or for their daughters to be soldiers: although I also know, some do. I mean that now they know they don't have to live the way they do. And so many of the world's women and their men do need, in fact, to live differently.

Civilization must be defended and equality means that those who benefit from it—should defend it.

As for Americans, we live now in a society where death in childbirth is so rare that we have been able to wipe the knowledge of its meaning from much of our collective memory, a society in which the human worth of women is now so great that we are almost full citizens.

From Chattel to Citizen

The formal, acknowledged participation of American women in combat as volunteer professionals will mark the near completion of women's transition from chattel to citizen. Until very recently [as of 2006], women lived in biological timelessness as chattels, if not outright slaves: we were extremely vulnerable to reproductive death and injury and had little control over our own bodies, especially concerning sex and reproduction. But since the Greeks, the citizen has been a man whose body was *his*, and so because his body was no one else's, the city's defense could be entrusted to him. And he lived with the consequences of his political choices. The feminist assertion that a woman's body is *hers*—period—full stop—is often called selfish. In fact, it is a necessary precondition for women to become citizens, to enter into normal historical, political and moral time and trade the high risks of reproductive chattel for the much lower, fundamentally chosen risks of the citizen. The citizen whose body is *hers* alone, and because it is *hers*, the nation can be entrusted to her defense.

If this strikes you as a strange thing to say, it is only the logical continuation of the American belief that the Republic must be defended by its citizens, whether professional or citizen soldiers, not mercenaries and slaves. Moreover, for many wars now, military service has been a fast track to citizenship for immigrants, and rightly so.

Now I wish to be explicit. Each of us must live within the limitations of our bodies, our intellects, our emotions. We can will ourselves to surpass and exceed our limits, but equality can only give us the opportunity to develop our wills. Equality is neither our desire to become more than we are nor our efforts to make ourselves so. Equality means only that women are not equal for the good things of civilization while being exempt from the hard and sometimes dangerous work of preserving it.

Civilization must be defended and equality means that those who benefit from it—should defend it. We women live in a Republic that increasingly recognizes our full civic and human worth. If the Republic goes down, so does our worth as citizens and human beings. Just as we have the citizen's civic right to participate in the common defense, limited only by our personal abilities, so we have the citizen's civic responsibility to provide for that defense, also limited only by our abilities—as part of the community to be defended.

The Republic, our Republic should be able to count upon us to fulfill that responsibility and exercise that right as citizens together.

12

To Be Draftable, Women Must Be Allowed in Combat

Kalamazoo Gazette

The following viewpoint was written by the editorial staff of the Kalamazoo Gazette, *a daily newspaper in Kalamazoo, Michigan.*

Women need and want equal treatment under the law. Further, full equity demands that women be eligible for any military draft that might be instituted in the future; however, the current combat exclusion law banning women from ground combat would deny women equal opportunity in the military into which they would be drafted. Consequently, women must be eligible for combat in order to be constitutionally eligible for the draft.

"Remember the Ladies." These famous words by Abigail Adams, wife of President John Adams, were written during the drafting of the Declaration of Independence as a plea to take women into consideration in the formation of our county.

Thus began women's suffrage.

Women have always been perceived as the inferior sex. However, women, being also capable-minded organisms, realized that equality was necessary. Abigail Adams started a revolution that grew into great controversies, protests, demonstrations and revelations. Women fought and still fight for equal rights, treatment, wages and opportunities. Women want equality, plain and simple.

Yet, when the issue of a draft being implemented arises, women would rather slide into the shadows and let the men serve our country. It is not right for women to only choose equality when it is convenient for us. Doesn't full citizenship come with full responsibility?

Now, the fact remains that women obviously do not have the same physical makeup as men. Men are innately stronger and can endure more physical work. Women are the natural nurturers of children and, thus, are needed to help repopulate society after such large numbers of casualties.

However, one could argue that with the new technology in the weaponry of warfare, that war is becoming more a challenge of the mind than the body. Since women have earned the title of being just as competent in mind as men, women should be just as capable of serving in a war as men.

[Because] of the many combat restrictions, women do not possess the same opportunities for promotion as their male counterparts.

Of course, the majority of women are uncomfortable with the thought of risking their lives out on the front lines, but the fact is men are too. War is a frightening event for everyone, but there is a common slogan in our country that states, "United We Stand," not "United We Stand (With Some Exceptions)."

When it comes to the draft, many people have very strong opinions. The general consensus is that women should be included in the draft. This stems from the idea of equality. With the notion of equal pay between the sexes and the outcry against gender discrimination in the workplace, it seems almost common sense for both sexes to be eligible for the draft. A closer look at military policy reveals that allowing women to be eligible for the draft would not promote equality at all.

Military policy excludes women from combat service with the statement: "Women may not be assigned to duty on vessels or in aircraft that are engaged in combat missions." When former president Jimmy Carter requested the authorization to register women for the draft, Congress determined that "any future draft would be characterized by a need for combat troops." If women are restricted from combat, and the purpose of a draft is to obtain combat troops, then why should women be included in the draft? U.S. Sen. Roger Jepsen, R-Iowa, said, "The shortage would be in the combat arms. That is why you have drafts."

Not only are women restricted from any combat missions, they also cannot receive the same promotions as men in the military. With regard to all of the many combat restrictions, women do not possess the same opportunities for promotion as their male counterparts. This supports the late U.S. Supreme Court Chief Justice William Rehnquist's statement: "Men and women are simply not similarly situated for purposes of a draft or registration for a draft."

These patriarchal values are the reason that, even today, women are prohibited from combat.

As a young woman, I believe that my possible inclusion in the draft would not promote equality. Rehnquist also said, "The starting point for any discussion of the appropriateness of registering women for the draft is the question of the proper role of women in combat."

Feminism has taught us a lot about a woman's competence. We've found that a woman won't inexplicably sprout a mustache if she plays a sport, that a woman has enough intellect to take on prestigious careers and that she has a purpose far beyond housewife and mother.

From tennis star Althea Gibson to astronaut Dr. Sally Ride, from U.S. Supreme Court Justice Sandra Day O'Connor to politician Shirley Chisholm, women have surpassed all expectations set by society, but we can't seem to shake the orthodox gender roles governing the way this culture thinks.

Women, the "nurturers," and men the "protectors." When the Equal Rights Amendment was being considered, people feared its ratification because they thought it would interfere with the woman as the homemaker and man as head of the household.

These patriarchal values are the reason that, even today, women are prohibited from combat.

The government wants to protect women from military violence, yet doesn't have a problem with the fact that 95 percent of domestic abuse victims are women along with 61 percent of those raped under age 18.

Then society doubts a woman's physical capabilities although according to British researcher Diane Hale, a woman is less likely to get fatigued and be less prone to muscle damage due to estrogen. Oxidization of fatty acids and balance are better in women, in addition to their ability to remain at high exertion level longer than men.

The war on terrorism is no privilege to participate in, but how can society even question a woman's adequacy anymore? With the beauty myth, domestic violence, rape, sexual harassment and sexual discrimination, don't women fight a war every day?

13

Women Should Not Be Drafted, Nor Allowed in Combat

Robert L. Maginnis

Robert L. Maginnis, a retired U.S. Army lieutenant colonel, works as a national security and foreign affairs analyst for radio and television.

The demand from the U.S. Army for more combat soldiers is leading inexorably toward the drafting of women for military service. In spite of the ban on women in combat, women are filling more and more roles on the battlefield. By allowing this, the United States demonstrates that it does not value women as child bearers or nurturers. In addition, women cause disruption and a lack of cohesion in combat units, making the units less prepared for battle. Women should not serve anywhere on a battlefield nor should they be conscripted for service.

"I just don't think America is ready to see a woman without an arm," said Juanita Wilson, an army staff sergeant who lost her hand to an improvised explosive device that destroyed her vehicle while on a mission in Iraq. Despite this statement, it seems that many in the United States have been coarsened to the killing and maiming of young women and are ready for more of the same. Thirty-five women have died and 271 have been wounded in Iraq [as of 2005].

Robert L. McGinnis, "Women on the Front Lines?," *The Washington Times*, May 15, 2005, p. A18. Copyright © 2005 The Washington Times LLC. All rights reserved. Reproduced by permission.

Sgt. Wilson is one of five American military women at Walter Reed hospital who have lost limbs during combat in Iraq.

Daughters Could Be Drafted

The sight of young women maimed in combat will become more common unless action is taken. Military bureaucrats, members of Congress and the media seem to be lusting for a more-women-in-combat policy that could lead to conscripting our daughters if a draft becomes necessary.

Rep. Heather Wilson, a 1980s Air Force veteran and New Mexico Republican, suggests the killing and maiming of young women in combat is now accepted by Americans. She told *The Washington Post*, "We have gotten beyond the point where losing a daughter is somehow worse than losing a son."

But Connie Halfaker, the mother of one of those women at Walter Reed recovering from a lost limb, trusted the Army's promise to keep women out of direct combat and never worried about her daughter going to war, although she told a reporter, "I knew it was a possibility that I would need to give up my son for a war." Lt. Dawn Halfaker, who lost her right arm on a military police patrol last year in Ba'qubah, Iraq, explained, "Women in combat is not really an issue. It is happening."

Although President Bush has said, "No women in combat," the enemy doesn't discriminate. Insurgents target every American, whether male, female, combatant or noncombatant.

The line defining combat is getting very fuzzy.

The fact is that the war in Iraq is unlike a conventional war. It is a struggle against well-armed insurgents with no clearly defined battle lines. It is a classic example of guerrilla warfare where no participant is safe.

Service Women Face Increased Danger

Today [in 2005], 15 percent of the active army are women. They pepper the ranks of all but direct combat units. Though as of 1994, women were barred from "units and positions required to collocate and remain with direct ground combat units assigned to direct ground combat missions," the Pentagon policy actually increases the danger for servicewomen.

Recently, Army Secretary Francis Harvey told Congress his women-in-combat policy doesn't need to be changed to comply with the 1994 provision. Perhaps, but the Army is assigning women to forward combat companies, which are in direct support of the 3rd Infantry Division's new brigade combat teams now serving in Baghdad. This potentially makes them increasingly vulnerable to attacks by insurgents.

Our young women are no longer valued as the bearers and nurturers of future generations. . . .

Even though women are not supposed to serve in combat they do fly Army helicopters in hostile areas. Maj. Ladda Duckworth lost both legs when a rocket-propelled grenade downed her Black Hawk helicopter last fall. Women also serve in multiple-launch rocket, reconnaissance and Stryker units. The line defining combat is getting very fuzzy.

The only way the United States can eliminate women from dying or being maimed in direct combat is to remove them from the battlefield. "That would be politically untenable," said a powerful congressman to this writer, and besides, it would force male soldiers to serve more frequent combat tours. The Army is dependent upon the large female force to perform global missions.

That fact sheds light on a hard reality. Our Army is straining for more soldiers to sustain operations across 120 nations with more than 303,000 forward deployed. The global war on terrorism is expected to last many years. Even though no one wants to conscript young people, the seriousness of the threat and the military's faltering recruiting efforts may intersect and lead inevitably to the drafting of women. The legal stage for such a scenario is being set as more and more women become engaged in combat. Conscription has always been an emergency provision to fill the military's ranks with combatants.

This nation should be ashamed it has bowed before political correctness and allowed the removal of barriers that protect our young women.

The coarsening of the United States on this issue is pitiful. Our young women are no longer valued as the bearers and nurturers of future generations—they are now interchangeable with men and expendable. I am pessimistic that Congress, which is constitutionally responsible for military personnel issues, will listen.

Women Should Not Be in Combat

Congress didn't listen when it was warned that introducing a small number of women into military units would cause disruption, lower morale and damage unit cohesion. Sexual misconduct in mixed-sex units has become the elephant in the living room for the modern military, but don't ask the PC brass.

Congress didn't listen when it was warned that young women have two-thirds the cardiovascular fitness and half the upper body strength of the average man. Our elected representatives allowed the Pentagon to gender norm physical requirements, producing a less ready force.

This nation should be ashamed it has bowed before political correctness and allowed the removal of barriers that protect our young women. There is no compelling national security reason for our daughters to serve in combat. There are many compelling reasons to deny them this deadly "opportunity."

Organizations to Contact

The editors have compiled the following list of organizations concerned with the issued debated in this book. The descriptions are derived from materials provided by the organizations. All have publications or information available for interested readers. The list was compiled as of the date of publication of the present volume; the information provided here may change. Be aware that many organizations take several weeks or longer to respond to inquiries so allow as much time as possible.

Air Force Association
1501 Lee Highway, Arlington, VA   22209-1198
Web site: www.afa.org

The Air Force Association (AFA) is an independent, nonprofit, civilian education organization promoting public understanding of aerospace power and the pivotal role it plays in the security of the nation. AFA publishes *Air Force Magazine*, conducts national symposia, and disseminates information through outreach programs. Its Web site also provides many useful links and publications about the Air Force in general and women in the Air Force in particular.

Association of the United States Army
2425 Wilson Blvd., Arlington, VA   22201
(800) 336-4570
e-mail: ausa-info@ausa.org
Web site: www.ausa.org

The Association of the United States Army is a private, nonprofit educational organization that provides support for the members of the U.S. Army, Army Reserves, National Guard, retirees, and family members. Their Web site offers a number of brochures and publications. In addition, the Association publishes a print magazine, *Army*, also accessible through the Web site.

Center for Military Readiness

P.O. Box 51600, Livonia, MI   48151
(202) 347-5333
e-mail: info@cmrlink
Web site: www.crmlink.org

Directed by Elaine Donnelly, the Center for Military Readiness is a nonpartisan, nonprofit educational organization whose stated purpose is to promote sound military personnel policies so that the U.S. military is always prepared to defend the country. The organization's Web site has information for students, including links to full text articles and essays.

Concerned Women for America

1015 Fifteenth St. NW, Suite 1100, Washington, DC   20005
(202) 488-7000 • fax: (202) 488-0806
Web site: www.cwfa.org

Concerned Women for America is a large public policy women's organization. Its stated mission is to protect and promote Biblical values among all citizens. The organization asserts that the United States has declining moral values and needs to return to Biblical principals. The organization provides brochures and articles on issues of importance to women, including women in combat.

Council on Biblical Manhood and Womanhood

2825 Lexington Road, Box 926, Louisville, KY   40280
(502) 897-4065 • fax: (502) 897-4061
e-mail: office@cbmw.org
Web site: www.cbmw.org

The Council on Biblical Manhood and Womanhood (CBMW) is a religious organization dedicated to the teachings of the Bible that point out the differences between men and women. A resolution from the CBMW offers scriptural evidence as a reason for opposing women in combat. The Web site offers resources concerning gender issues as they relate to evangelical Christians, including the role of women in the military.

Independent Women's Forum

1726 M St. NW, Tenth Floor, Washington, DC   20036
(202) 419-1820
e-mail: info@iwf.org
Web site: www.iwf.org

The Independent Women's Forum is a nonprofit, nonpartisan organization whose stated mission is "to rebuild civil society by advancing economic liberty, personal responsibility, and political freedom." Generally, the Independent Women's Forum opposes feminism. Their Web site provides information and links on national security, including issues of women in the military and in combat.

Minerva Center

20 Granada Road, Pasadena, MD   21122
(410) 897-0929
Web site: www.minervacenter.com

The Minerva Center is a nonprofit educational organization. Its role is to provide information and research on women and the military and women in war. The group publishes *Minerva Journal of Women and War*. The Minerva Center is non-partisan and does not advocate for any position. The group offers a discussion group, H-Minerva on the H-Net discussion network as well as a range of publications available through their Web site.

National Organization for Women

1100 H St. NW, Third Floor, Washington, DC   20005
(202) 628-8669 • fax: (202) 785-8576
e-mail: now@now.org
Web site: www.now.org

The National Organization for Women (NOW) is the largest organization of feminists in the United States. Its stated goals are to bring about equality for all women. The group has taken an official stand that the combat restriction ban for women is discriminatory. The NOW Web site offers many articles and resources for students studying women's issues in general and women in combat in particular.

National Women's Law Center
11 Dupont Circle NW, Suite 800, Washington, DC   20036
(202) 588-5180 • fax: (202) 588-5185
e-mail: info@nwlc.org
Web site: www.nwlc.org

The National Women's Law Center (NWLC) is a nonpartisan, nonprofit organization. It works to expand opportunities for women and girls by advocating for new laws, litigating cases, and providing education about the law. The NWLC Web site has information concerning important issues for women, including employment discrimination and the ban on women in combat.

U.S. Department of Defense
1000 Defense Pentagon, Washington, DC   20301-1000
Web site: www.defenselink.mil

The U.S. Department of Defense (DoD), located in the Pentagon in Washington, DC, is the headquarters for not only the Secretary of Defense and his staff, but also for all branches of the U.S. armed services. The DoD Web site, *Defenselink*, provides an enormous amount of information, including important publications, news stories, policy updates, and contact information. In addition, it provides links to each branch of the armed services and to the Defense Technical Center, a source of additional publications. *Defenselink* is a vital tool for anyone studying any topic concerning the military, including women in combat.

U.S. Navy
Department of the Navy, Washington, DC   20350-1200
Web site: www.navy.mil

The U.S. Navy supplies on its Web site information concerning careers, news, navy history, and fact files. During Women's

History Month, it usually features women in the U.S. Navy as a news story. In addition, the site offers links to other military branches and pertinent information regarding women in combat.

Women's e-News
135 W. 29th Street, Suite 1005, New York, NY   10001
(212) 244-1720 • fax: (212) 244-2320
e-mail: editors@womensenews.org
Web site: www.womensenews.org

Women's e-News is a clearinghouse for news about women from around the world. Its purpose is to provide a women's perspective on public policy issues. In addition to publishing full-text news articles on its Web site, it also provides many links, notably to information on women in combat and in the military.

Bibliography

Books

Rick Bragg   *I Am a Soldier, Too: The Jessica Lynch Story.* New York: Alfred A. Knopf, 2003.

Kingsley Browne   *Co-ed Combat: The New Evidence that Women Shouldn't Fight the Nation's Wars.* New York: Sentinel, 2007.

Katherine M. Cook   *Leading Soldiers on Today's Battlefield: Considerations on Contributions and Challenges of the Integration and Role of Soldiers Who Are Women.* Carlisle, PA: U.S. Army War College, 2006.

Maureen Dowd   *Are Men Necessary? When Sexes Collide.* New York: G.P. Putman's Sons, 2005.

Philip Gold   *The Coming Draft: The Crisis in Our Military and Why Selective Service Is Wrong for America.* New York: Presidio Press, 2006.

Heather Hasan   *American Women of the Gulf War.* New York: Rosen Publishing Group, 2004.

Joan Huber   *On the Origins of Gender Inequality.* Boulder, CO: Paradigm, 2007.

David Jones   *Women Warriors: A History.* Washington, DC: Brassey, 2003.

Janis L. Karpinski   *One Woman's Army: The Command-*
with Steven   *ing General of Abu Ghraib Tells Her*
Strasser   *Story.* New York: Miramax, 2005.

Tara McKelvey,   *One of the Guys: Women as Aggressors*
ed.   *and Torturers.* Emeryville, CA: Seal
                     Press, 2007.

Theodore   *Trained to Kill: Soldiers at War.* Balti-
Nadelson   more, MD: Johns Hopkins University
                     Press, 2005.

Kate O'Beirne   *Women Who Make the World Worse:*
                     And How Their Radical Feminist As-
                     sault Is Ruining Our Families, Mili-
                     tary, Schools, and Sports. New York:
                     Sentinel, 2006.

Lindy Pavkovich   *My Mom Wears Combat Boots.*
                     Bloomington, IN: 1st Books Library,
                     2004.

Steven Pressfield   *The Afghan Campaign.* New York:
                     Doubleday, 2006.

Erin Solaro   *Women in the Line of Fire: What You*
                     Should Know About Women in the
                     Military. Emeryville, CA: Seal Press,
                     2006.

Susan R. Sowers   *Women Combatants in World War I:*
                     A Russian Case Study. Carlisle, PA:
                     U.S. Army War College, 2003.

Brian Williams   *Life as a Fighter Pilot.* Chicago: Hei-
                     nemann Library, 2006.

Kayla Williams with Michael E. Staub   *Love My Rifle More than You: Young and Female in the U.S. Army.* New York: Norton, 2005.

James E. Wise Jr. and Scott Baron   *Women at War: Iraq, Afghanistan, and Other Conflicts.* Annapolis, MD: U.S. Naval Institute Press, 2006.

Sara L. Zeigler and Gregory G. Gunderson   *Moving beyond G.I. Jane: Women and the U.S. Military.* Lanham, MD: University Press of America, 2005.

Periodicals

Martha Ackman   "House Respects Women by Refusing to Limit Women in Combat," *U.S. Newswire,* May 27, 2005.

Lizette Alvarez   "Women at War: Officially, American Women Can't Serve in Combat, But in Iraq and Afghanistan, They're Fighting—and Dying—As Never Before," *New York Times Upfront,* March 12, 2007.

Scott Baldauf   "In Taliban Territory, GI Janes Give Afghans a Different View," *Christian Science Monitor,* November 4, 2003.

Frederick Barnes   "Women in Combat," *Defense & Foreign Affairs' Strategic Policy,* July 2005.

Janie Blankenship   "Women Change Face of Military," *VFW: Veterans of Foreign Wars,* March 2004.

Rosa Brooks | "In Defense of Women in Combat," *Los Angeles Times*, July 3, 2005.

Mona Charen | "Why Does the United States Put Its Mothers into Combat?" *Insight on the News*, April 29, 2003.

Sharon Cohen | "From Skies to Streets, Women Warriors Face the Enemy and Change Military Landscape," *USA Today*, December 3, 2006.

Kevin Diaz | "Should Women Be Shielded from Combat?" *Star Tribune*, May 20, 2005.

Elaine Donnelly | "Stealth Plan for Women in Combat," *Washington Times*, May 8, 2005.

Kim Dougherty | "From Support to Combat—Women in Military Aviation," *Women and Gender Studies Newsletter*, March 2004.

Tim Dyhouse | "Women in Combat Arms De-Emphasized," *VFW: Veterans of Foreign Wars*, May 2002.

Philip Gold and Erin Solaro | "Facts about Women in Combat Elude the Right," *Seattle Post-Intelligencer*, May 18, 2005.

Douglas Hanson | "Another Clinton Legacy," *American Thinker*, June 2, 2005.

Frederick J. Kroesen | "Women in Combat," *Army*, May 2006.

Gordon Lubold   "Coed Combat: Marines Rely on
                       Army Lionesses to Get the Job
                       Done," *Air Force Times*, August 16,
                       2004.

Julie Macur   "In the Line of Fire: Officially,
                       American Women Do Not Serve in
                       Combat Roles, But in Iraq, They're
                       on the Front Lines as Never Before,"
                       New York Times Upfront, January 20,
                       2006.

Tim McGurk   "Crossing the Lines," *Time*, February
                       27, 2006.

George Neumayr   "Equality Equals Death," *American
                       Spectator*, August 2004.

Kate O'Beirne   "An Army of Jessicas: About Women
                       in Combat: Let's Fight. Hard," *National Review*, May 19, 2003.

Mackubin   "A Man's Job," *National Review*, May
Thomas Owens   12, 2005.

Mackubin   "GI Jane, Again," *National Review*,
Thomas Owens   June 6, 2005.

Kathleen Parker   "Putting Women in Combat: The
                       Mother of Blunders," *Washington
                       Post*, April 7, 2007.

Jonathan B.   "Women in the Military: New Per-
Perlin, Susan H.   spectives, New Science," *Journal of
Mather, and   Women's Health*, November 2005.
Carole L. Turner

Cheryl L. Reed   "War Stress Heavier on Women,"
                       Chicago Sun Times, May 8, 2005.

Jennie Ruby   "Women in Combat Roles: Is That
                             the Question?" *off our backs*, Novem-
                             ber–December 2005.

Taryn McCall   "Feminists in the Military: Is Armed
Runck   Service Compatible with Feminism?"
                             off our backs, February 2006.

Amy Schlesing   "Women's Jobs Open Up in War;
                             Men-only Tradition Beginning to
                             Wane," *Arkansas Democrat-Gazette*,
                             October 22, 2006.

R. Claire Snyder   "The Citizen Soldier Tradition and
                             Gender Integration of the U.S. Mili-
                             tary," *Armed Forces & Society*, Winter
                             2003.

Ann Scott Tyson   "More Objections to Women-in-
                             Combat Ban," *Washington Post*, May
                             18, 2005.

USA Today   "Sharp-shooting Women Best Soviet
                             Snipers," December 1, 2006.

Wilma Vaught   "Should Women Be Allowed in Com-
and Elaine   bat? Women Make Up 15 Percent of
Donnelly   America's Armed Forces, But Military
                             Policy Prohibits Them from Serving
                             in Combat Zones," *New York Times
                             Upfront*, September 5, 2005.

George Wallace   "Emasculating the Military: Politi-
                             cally Correct Dictates Are Ever More
                             Being Imposed on Today's Military,
                             Degrading Morale, Discipline, and
                             Combat Effectiveness," *New Ameri-
                             can*, May 30, 2005.

Judith Webb   "Why Women Should Not Be on the Front Line," *Daily Mail*, June 4, 2007.

Jodi Wilgoren   "A New War Brings New Roles for Women," *New York Times*, March 28, 2003.

Index